NEW VANGUARD 302

TANKS IN THE BATTLE OF GERMANY 1945

Western Front

STEVEN J. ZALOGA   ILLUSTRATED BY FELIPE RODRÍGUEZ

OSPREY PUBLISHING

Bloomsbury Publishing Plc

Kemp House, Chawley Park, Cumnor Hill, Oxford OX2 9PH, UK

29 Earlsfort Terrace, Dublin 2, Ireland

1385 Broadway, 5th Floor, New York, NY 10018, USA

E-mail: info@ospreypublishing.com

www.ospreypublishing.com

OSPREY is a trademark of Osprey Publishing Ltd

First published in Great Britain in 2022

A catalogue record for this book is available from the British Library.

ISBN: PB 9781472848116; eBook: 9781472848123; ePDF 9781472848130; XML: 9781472848147

22 23 24 25 26   10 9 8 7 6 5 4 3 2

Index by Mark Swift
Typeset by PDQ Digital Media Solutions, Bungay, UK
Printed and bound in India by Replika Press Private Ltd.

FSC
MIX
Paper from responsible sources
FSC® C016779
www.fsc.org

Osprey Publishing supports the Woodland Trust, the UK's leading woodland conservation charity.

To find out more about our authors and books visit

www.ospreypublishing.com. Here you will find extracts, author interviews, details of forthcoming events and the option to sign up for our newsletter.

ACKNOWLEDGEMENTS

The author would like to thank Peter Brown and Timm Haasler for their help on this book. Unless otherwise noted, the photos here are primarily from official US sources, especially the US Army Signal Corps.

GLOSSARY

6th Army Group	Lt Gen. Jacob Devers' American/French force
12th Army Group	Gen. Omar Bradley's US force
21st Army Group	Field Marshal Bernard Montgomery's British/Canadian force
AFV	Armored Fighting Vehicle
GFM	*Generalfeldmarschall*
Heeresgruppe	Army Group, consisting of several field armies
HVAP	high-velocity, armor piercing (projectile)
KStN	*Kriegsstärkenachweisungen:* (war-establishment strength)
OB West	*Oberbefehlshaber West* (High Command West (Model's HQ))
Panzerjäger	tank destroyer
s.Pz.Abt.	*schwere Panzer Abteilung*: (heavy tank battalion)
s.Pz.Jg.Abt.	*schwere Panzerjäger Abteilung*: (heavy tank destroyer battalion)
Sturmgeschütz	assault gun
Wehrmacht	(German) armed forces

CONTENTS

INTRODUCTION   4

THE CAMPAIGN   4

DOCTRINE AND ORGANIZATION   13
- Wehrmacht
- US Army
- British/Canadian Armies

TECHNICAL FACTORS   26
- Wehrmacht
- US Army
- British/Canadian Armies

BATTLE ANALYSIS   44

FURTHER READING   47

INDEX   48

TANKS IN THE BATTLE OF GERMANY 1945

Western Front

INTRODUCTION

The final battle for Germany in 1945 pitted a declining Wehrmacht against foes from both east and west. This is the first book of a two-part series covering the *Westfront* (Western Front); the second book covers the *Ostfront* (Russian Front). It surveys the principal tank types on both sides, as well as tank surrogates such as the tank destroyer(*Panzerjäger*), and the assault gun (*Sturmgeschütz*). Due to space limitations, it does not cover self-propelled field artillery or light armored vehicles, such as armored cars and half-tracks. For convenience sake, in this book AFV (Armored Fighting Vehicle) refers to the tank surrogates, such as assault guns and tank destroyers.

THE CAMPAIGN

The success of the 1944 summer offensive pushed the Allied armies much further east than anticipated in the Operation *Overlord* plans, straining their supply chain. Gen. Dwight Eisenhower, supreme commander of the

An M4A1 of Co. F, 33rd Armored Regiment, Combat Command B, 3rd Armored Division passes by a knocked-out PzKpfw IV Ausf. G, probably from the 11.Panzer-Division, in Bad Marienburg on March 28, 1945 during the breakout from the Remagen bridgehead. The M4A1 is a survivor from the Normandy campaign and has a large steel plate added to the hull front, a modification on many 3rd Armored Division tanks following the capture of Cologne earlier in the month.

Allied Expeditionary Force, decided to continue a limited campaign along the German frontier in the autumn of 1944 to prevent the Wehrmacht from recovering. By October 1944, the expectation was that the main Allied offensive towards the Rhine would begin in early 1945 once adequate supplies had been amassed.

In late 1944, Generalfeldmarschall Walter Model's OB West (*Oberbefehlshaber West* (High Command West)) controlled three army groups. The northern-most, Heeresgruppe H, corresponded roughly to Field Marshal Bernard Montgomery's 21st Army Group, and was stationed in the Netherlands and northern Germany. The largest concentration of the Wehrmacht in the West was Heeresgruppe B, facing Gen. Omar Bradley's 12th Army Group from the Belgian border to the Saar industrial region. The southern-most force was Heeresgruppe G in the Saar/Alsace region, facing Jacob Devers' US/French 6th Army Group.

The British/Canadian 21st Army Group spent most of the autumn of 1944 dealing with German defenses in the Scheldt estuary to clear the waterways to the critical port of Antwerp. Although Antwerp had been liberated by the British Army in September 1944, the estuary leading to the port had remained in German hands. Canadian forces overcame the defenses on the south bank of the Scheldt in October 1944, leading to a British amphibious operation, November 3–8, 1944, to overcome the heavily fortified defenses of Walcheren island. Tank operations on both sides were limited by the marshy terrain in this campaign.

Bradley's 12th Army Group was the first Allied force to reach the German frontier in September 1944. It captured Aachen on October 21, the first major German city to fall to Allied forces. In mid-November, Bradley planned a major offensive, codenamed Operation *Queen*, to push over the Roer river. It stalled in the face of unexpectedly strong German resistance, including significant Panzer reinforcements. Unbeknown to Bradley, the Germans were massing forces in this sector for a planned Ardennes offensive in December 1944.

A Panther Ausf. G from II./Pz.Lehr Rgt.130, Panzer-Lehr Division knocked out by bazooka fire by Co. A, 1/393rd Infantry, 99th Division near Ginsterhahn during the fighting for the Remagen bridgehead on March 11, 1945. Korpsgruppe Bayerlein counterattacked the 99th Division shortly after it had crossed the Rhine near Linz with less than a dozen tanks.

A Valentine 17pdr of the 102nd (Northumberland Hussars) Anti-Tank Regiment, supporting the 2nd Gordon Highlanders of the 15th Scottish Division, 30th Corps near Nütterden, Germany to the east of Kleve on February 10, 1945 during Operation *Veritable*. This tank destroyer, later called the 'Archer', was used by the antitank units of British infantry divisions in 1945 while the M10 17pdr was used in the armoured divisions.

Though often overlooked, Lt Gen. Jacob Devers' US/French 6th Army Group was by far the most successful Allied formation in the autumn of 1944. Its Seventh US Army managed to fight its way over the Vosges mountains in November 1944, capturing the provincial capital of Strasbourg and reaching the Rhine river by mid-December. The First French Army pushed along the French–Swiss frontier near Basel, reaching the Rhine in the Belfort gap area during the November–December fighting. Opposing Panzer forces in this sector were meager.

On December 16, 1944, the Wehrmacht surprised the US Army in the Ardennes. The focal point of the attack towards the Elsenborn ridge and Antwerp failed within the first week, dooming the operation before Christmas. The offensive made modest gains towards secondary objectives such as Bastogne. It took until mid-January 1945 for Bradley's 12th Army Group to recover all of the lost terrain. The Ardennes was Hitler's desperate gamble to regain the strategic initiative in the West. The Wehrmacht expended most of its Panzer reserves in the attack, leaving it considerably weakened in the aftermath of its defeat. Hitler followed the Ardennes offensive with several smaller attacks in the Saar/Alsace region against the 6th Army Group, starting with Operation *Nordwind* on New Year's Eve. These also failed, and cost Heeresgruppe G most of its Panzer resources.

Panzer strength in the West, January 15, 1945						
	Pz.II/III	Pz.IV	Panther	Tiger	StuG	Total
Norway/Denmark						
Operational	89	30				**119**
In repair	9	2				**11**
West						
Operational	35	330	221	64	340	**990**
In repair	10	264	266	46	375	**961**
In delivery		172	146	7	263	**588**
Southwest (Italy)						
Operational	27	134	17	32	265	**475**
In repair	8	28	9	4	80	**129**
In delivery		17			17	**34**
Western fronts (totals)						
Operational	151	494	238	96	605	**1,584**
In repair	27	294	275	50	455	**1,101**
In delivery		189	146	7	280	**622**
Total	**178**	**977**	**659**	**153**	**1,340**	**3,307**

One reason that the Wehrmacht had been able to mass its Panzer reserves for the Ardennes offensive was that the Red Army had been relatively quiet on its main front nearest Berlin. The Soviet army, like the western Allies, had outrun its logistical tail by the late summer of 1944.

It had spent most of the autumn building up for a final 1945 offensive. In the interim, the Red Army remained active in peripheral theaters such as Hungary and Kurland. In late 1944, Panzer forces in the East had been starved of new equipment in favor of amassing two Panzer armies for the Ardennes attack.

On January 12, 1945, shortly before the conclusion of the Ardennes fighting, the Red Army launched its massive Vistula–Oder offensive aimed at Berlin. With limited resources, the Wehrmacht could no longer fight a two-front war. Berlin was forced to re-balance its Panzer forces from west to east. The 6.SS-Panzer-Army was pulled out of Belgium and sent east. Likewise, Panzer forces committed to the Alsace/Saar offensives, such as 10.SS-Panzer-Division, were also transferred east to face the Red Army.

Panzer Strength: East vs. West 15 January 1945			
	West	East	Total
Operational Panzer	979	1,175	**2,154**
Panzer in Repair	646	589	**1,235**
Panzer in delivery	342	486	**828**
Operational Stug	605	1,820	**2,425**
Stug in Repair	455	402	**857**
Stug in delivery	280	434	**714**
Total	**3,307**	**4,906**	**8,266**

As a result of this strategic shift, Wehrmacht strength on the Russian Front increased from 3,784 tanks and AFVs on January 5 to 4,906 on January 15. The Panzer balance continued to shift in favor of the Russian front through the rest of 1945, while strength in the West continued to decline. For example, in November–December 1944 a total of 2,197 new Panzers and AFVs were delivered to the West compared to only 919 in the East. However, from January to March 1945 after the Ardennes offensive, the trend reversed with the West receiving only 544 Panzers and AFVs compared 3,086 in the East.

Distribution of new Panzers and AFVs: Nov 1944–Mar 10, 1945						
West	Nov	Dec	Jan	Feb	Mar	total
Pz.IV	205	47	58			**310**
Pz.IV Lg (A)	49		25			**74**
Pz.IV Lg (V)	135	128	17			**280**
Panther	281	191	85	1		**558**
Tiger	26	6	6		13	**51**
StuG	382	261	82		88	**813**
Jagdpanzer 38	218	137	24	40		**419**
Jagdpanther	20	49	36	20	5	**130**
Jagdtiger	9	16	6	6	14	**51**
Sturmpanzer	20	17	4		14	**55**
Total	**1,345**	**852**	**343**	**67**	**134**	**2,741**

By the time that the Allies initiated new operations in February 1945, the tank balance in the West was skewed heavily against the Wehrmacht. Only about 900 Panzers and AFVs faced 4,400 British/Canadian tanks and AFVs plus 12,200 US tanks and AFVs, an imbalance of 1 to 18. The imbalance

An 8.8cm PaK43/1 Nashorn of s.Panzerjäger Abt. 654, knocked out in a duel with a French M10 3in GMC tank destroyer of the French 2e Division Blindée during the fighting near Riedwihr on January 26 in the Elsenheim woods during the final skirmishes to overcome the Colmar pocket in Alsace. This was one of six that that were lost that day.

continued to worsen through the spring of 1945, reaching its nadir in April–May 1945 at less than 1 to 60.

The Rhine was Germany's last major strategic barrier to the Allied advance in the West. On February 8, Montgomery's 21st Army Group initiated Operation *Veritable*, its first major operation on German soil in 1945. This British/Canadian offensive pushed across the Dutch frontier into the Reichswald, a heavily forested area southwest of Kleve. The offensive was agonizingly slow due to determined German resistance and the sodden ground conditions. Panzer formations in this sector were very weak; the 116.Panzer-Division had only six operational PzKpfw IVs and 10 Panthers. *Veritable* was followed on February 20 with Operation *Blockbuster* that pushed to the southeast, reaching the Rhine near Xanten. On March 9, Berlin gave 1.Fallschirm-Armee permission to withdraw over the Rhine.

Eisenhower had planned to deploy the Ninth US Army to assist Operation *Veritable* on February 10. However, the Germans opened up the Roer river dams, flooding the Roer plains. As a result, Operation *Grenade* was delayed until February 23 to allow the plains to dry out enough for mechanized operations. Once started, these attacks progressed so well that on March 1, Lt Gen. William Simpson, commander of Ninth US Army, suggested a hasty Rhine crossing near Düsseldorf. Montgomery refused, favoring an intricately planned river crossing operation three weeks later, code-named Operation *Varsity-Plunder*.

OB West Panzer Strength, 5 February 1945		
	Operational	**Total***
Pz.III/IV	68	110
Panther	96	219
Tiger	26	61
7.5cm Sfl	48	101
Jagdpanther	43	66
Jagdtiger	21	28
Nashorn	8	12
Stug/Jagdpanzer	568	1,009
Stu.Panzer	15	32
Total	**893**	**1,638**
*Includes operational vehicles plus those in repair/damaged		

Early March saw the two US army groups closing on the Rhine. First US Army began Operation *Lumberjack*, clearing the west bank of the Rhine from Cologne southward while the 6th Army Group launched Operation *Undertone* from the Wissembourg gap up along the Rhine. The March campaign was based on the premise that the American Rhine crossings would wait until after

Montgomery's forces jumped the Rhine with Operation *Varsity-Plunder*. The main American objective was to trap and destroy as many German units as possible along the western bank of the Rhine and before they could escape over the river. Hitler's adamant refusal to permit withdrawals only hastened the demise of the Wehrmacht in the West. By this stage of the war, nearly all of the major Rhine bridges had been knocked down by Allied air attack or demolished by German units after they withdrew over the Rhine.

A pair of M4A3E2 assault tanks of the 746th Tank Battalion support the weary GIs of the 39th Infantry, 9th Division near Rath on February 27, 1945 during the final push for the Roer dams through the Hürtgen forest.

German Panzer strength continued to deteriorate through early 1945 due to the lack of replacement vehicles. By mid-March, OB West only had 316 tanks of which only 107 (34%) were operational and the rest battle-damaged or in repair. The British/Canadian 21st Army Group was facing only two major Panzer formations, 15.Panzer-Grenadier-Division and 116.Panzer-Division with only 26 operational tanks combined. The bulk of the German Panzer force was in Heeresgruppe B, facing Bradley's 12th Army Group, but with only 79 operational tanks. Heeresgruppe G, facing the 6th Army Group in the Saar region only had the 17.SS-Pz.Grenadier-Division, equipped mainly with assault guns and only 2 tanks.

Strength of major Panzer units of OB West, March 15, 1945*								
	Pz.IV	Pz.IV/70	Panther	Tiger	StuG	Flak Pz.	Total	Operational
Herresgruppe H								
116.Pz.Div.	2+4	4+3	8+24		2+9	5+5	66	21
15.Pz.Gren.Div.	2+1	10+11			8+6	0+2	40	20
Heeresgruppe B								
2.Pz.Div.	4+12		4+31		2+20	3+2	78	13
9.Pz.Div.	1+4	3+5	10+8		2+0	0+4	37	16
11.Pz.Div.	4+13		14+19		2+4	4+7	67	24
Pz.Lehr.Div.	2+4	6+8	13+16			1+1	**51**	**22**
3.Pz.Gren.Div.	1+0	6+14			4+5		**30**	**11**
Pz.Bde.106	1+2	4+3	0+5			2+1	**18**	**7**
Pz.Abt.Fkl.301				4+9			**13**	**4**
s.H.Pz.Abt.506				2+13			**15**	**2**
Heeresgruppe G								
17.SS-Pz.Gren.Div.	2+0				47+15	4+0	**68**	**53**
Total	**59**	**77**	**152**	**28**	**126**	**41**	**483**	
Operational	**19**	**33**	**49**	**6**	**67**	**19**		**193**
Operational + In repair/damaged								

The 12.8cm Jagdtiger 3./s. Panzerjäger-Abteilung 653 commanded by Feldwebel Heinz Telgmann and burned out near Morsbronn-les-Bains in Alsace. Five of the battalion's Jagdtigers departed their assembly area on the evening of March 16, 1945 to attack the US 103rd Infantry Division positions in Morsbronn. They were attacked by rocket-firing P-47 Thunderbolts and artillery. Three Jagdtigers were lost due to a combination of battle damage and mechanical breakdown.

On March 7, the US 9th Armored Division arrived near Remagen to discover that the Ludendorff railroad bridge was still standing. The bridge was quickly seized, giving the First US Army a toehold on the east bank of the Rhine. Eisenhower ordered the bridgehead to be reinforced, but still waited for *Varsity-Plunder* as the main Rhine crossing effort. On March 12, Patton's Third US Army launched its local offensive in the Saar-Palatinate. Opposing German forces had already been crushed to the north and south by *Lumberjack* and *Undertone*, and the German defense quickly disintegrated. This led to the so-called "Rhine Rat Race" as Patton's armored divisions charged ahead against retreating German units. On reaching the Rhine, Patton staged a hasty crossing on March 22 near Oppenheim, followed by additional Rhine crossings over the following week. By month's end, Patton had reached Frankfurt.

Montgomery's 21st Army Group launched Operation *Varsity-Plunder* on March 23–24 north of Wesel, against very weak opposition by the 86.Korps. The only Panzer forces in the region were the weak 15.Panzer-Grenadier-Division and the battered 116. Panzer-Division. This enormous airborne–amphibious–ground operation included one of the few uses of airborne tanks when a handful of Locust light tanks were landed by Hamilcar gliders as part of Operation *Varsity-Plunder*. The Ninth US Army launched a subsidiary mission codenamed Operation *Flashpoint* to push over the Rhine south of the British attack.

Although Eisenhower had originally supported the scheme to concentrate on the British Operation *Varsity-Plunder* as the

The Churchill infantry tank served as the basis for the Churchill Crocodile flamethrower tank, which towed a special trailer for the fuel and compressed air. This was one of the types employed by the 79th Armoured Division "Hobart's Funnies," and one is seen here in the Oberhausen-Sterkrade area on March 31, 1945 with smoke billowing from a nearby synthetic oil refinery.

focus for the Rhine campaign, the success of the various US field armies, and especially the Remagen bridgehead, led him to reconsider. He reverted to his preferred strategic approach of a broad, multi-army advance.

On March 25, Bradley's 12th Army Group launched Operation *Voyage*. The northern prong of the attack was a drive by Simpson's Ninth US Army along the northern side of the Ruhr industrial belt, while First US Army attacked out of the Remagen bridgehead, aiming for the southern side of the Ruhr. Patton's Third US Army

began an even deeper envelopment from further south. The rapid progress of these spearheads in the final days of March led Bradley to propose enveloping the Ruhr between Ninth and First US Armies.

The remaining strength of Heeresgruppe B was concentrated in the Ruhr sector including most of the Panzer force. By this stage, Panzer strength in the West was meager, only 47 operational tanks on April 10, 1945. Indeed, there was greater Panzer strength in peripheral theaters such as Italy and Norway. One of the few tank battles of the 1945 spring campaigns took place in the final days of March when Gen. Fritz Bayerlein's 53.Armee-Korps staged a counterattack against the US Army's VII Corps around the Panzer training grounds at Paderborn, attempting to prevent the encirclement of the Ruhr. These attacks were crushed, and elements of the 2nd Armored Division (Ninth US Army) and 3rd Armored Division (First US Army) met on April 1, 1945 near Lippstadt, closing the trap around the Ruhr.

A column of Sherman V DD amphibious tanks of the Staffordshire Yeomanry, with their floatation skirts retracted, move through the town of Lauenberg during the Elbe river crossing on April 29, 1945. This was part of the battle for Hamburg by XII Corps, Second British Army in the concluding weeks of the war.

Operational Panzer strength in the West, April 10, 1945					
	West	Norway	Denmark	Southwest	Total
Pz.III		70	20	49	**139**
Pz.IV	11		9	119	**139**
Pz.IV/70	2			8	**10**
Panther	24			23	**47**
Tiger	10			22	**32**
Beute Pz.		79			**79**
StuG.III	29	14	27	109	**179**
Stug.IV	32		7	16	**55**
StuH				29	**29**
Beute StuG	67			144	**211**
Jagd.Pz.38	70		1	64	**135**
Nashorn	10			71	**81**
Jagdpanther	5				**5**
Jagdtiger	24				**24**
Flak Pz.	6		4		**10**
BergePz.	3			11	**14**
Total	**293**	**163**	**68**	**665**	**1,189**

ABOVE LEFT
A Panther Ausf. G
Panzerbefehlswagen from
I./Pz.Lehr-Rgt.130, Panzer Lehr
Division seen here abandoned
in Krefeld after the city's
capture by the 2nd Armored
Division on March 3, 1945.
This tank was built by MAN in
November–December 1944.
Curiously enough, it has the
fittings for the special box on
the upper right of the rear plate
intended for infrared night
vision equipment. Contrary to
legend, there is no evidence
that IR-equipped Panthers saw
combat in the West in 1945.

ABOVE RIGHT
A Jagdpanther of 1./s.
Panzerjäger Abt. 654, one of
three knocked out by M36
90mm GMC tank destroyers
of the 899th Tank Destroyer
Battalion attached to the
9th Infantry Division during
fighting near Kaimig-
Ginsterhain on March 13, 1945.

Bradley assumed that the Wehrmacht had evacuated the Ruhr and anticipated that only about 70,000 troops remained. In fact, Hitler had refused GFM Walter Model's plea to withdraw Heeresgruppe B from the Ruhr. The Ruhr pocket held out until April 18 with the surrender of about 317,000 German troops; this was a larger bag of prisoners than Stalingrad or Tunisia. Model committed suicide rather than surrender.

The destruction of Heeresgruppe B ended any coordinated German defense in the West for the last three weeks of the war. The new OB West commander, GFM Albert Kesselring, referred to the final battles as the "makeshift campaign." Berlin ordered numerous preposterous counterattacks based on fantasy paper formations. There were scattered encounters between Allied and German armored vehicles, but usually involving only a handful of German AFVs.

Although Montgomery proposed a lightning armored thrust to reach Berlin, Eisenhower refused on the grounds that Roosevelt, Churchill, and Stalin had already agreed at the Yalta conference to place Berlin in the Soviet occupation zone.

One of the new T26E3 Pershing
heavy tanks of the 9th Armored
Division passes through the
ruins of Euskirchen on March
5, 1945 during Operation
Lumberjack.

The final campaigns in late April involved four major operations. First Canadian Army was assigned to liberate the Netherlands as quickly as possible due to widespread civilian suffering from severe winter food shortages. The British Second Army was directed northeast to seize the German North Sea ports. The final phase of the British advance, codenamed Operation *Enterprise*, had the strategic objective to race to the Baltic sea thereby pre-empting the Soviet occupation of Denmark.

An M4 medium tank of the 7th Armored Division dips its tracks into the Baltic along the north eastern German coast near Wismar on May 3, 1945. The US XVIII Airborne Corps formed the extreme eastern wing of the advance of Montgomery's 21st Army Group, intending to seal off the Danish border before the advance of the Red Army.

In the center, the First and Ninth US Armies were instructed to advance to the Elbe river to meet the Red Army. This objective was reached first on April 25 by the 69th Infantry Division, followed by other US and Soviet units through early May. The fourth major operation to the south involved Patton's Third US Army and Devers' 6th Army Group. These formations cleared southern Germany with the aim of preventing the formation of an "Alpine Redoubt" by die-hard Nazis. This threat proved to be ephemeral. In the event, the southern drive linked up 6th Army Group along the Italian border with Gen. Mark Clark's 15th Army Group coming north out of Italy though the Alpine passes. Patton's Third US Army advanced the deepest of all of Eisenhower's formations, reaching into Austria and Czechoslovakia. With the collapse of the Third Reich, these were the last major actions by the Allies in the West.

DOCTRINE AND ORGANIZATION

Wehrmacht

The Panzer units available to OB West in February 1945 were considerably diminished from the force available for the Ardennes offensive due to the transfer of the 6.SS-Panzer-Armee to the Russian Front in mid-January 1945. This also led to an almost total removal of Waffen-SS Panzer units from the West. The sole exception was 17.SS-Panzergrenadier-Division "Götz von Berlichingen," a second-rate unit that was assigned to Heeresgruppe G in the Saar region. As a result, almost all OB West Panzer units were regular army (Heer) formations.

In early February 1945, OB West had five Panzer divisions (2., 9.,11.,116., Panzer-Lehr) and three Panzergrenadier divisions (3., 15., and 17.SS). These were nominally under the 1944 KStN organizations, though all of these divisions were short of personnel and equipment at the time. Tank strength was especially weak with the divisions averaging only about 65 tanks each, both operational and in repair, or roughly 40 percent of the authorized 165 tanks. The situation was made far worse by the poor maintenance conditions of the tanks due to their mechanical exhaustion from the Ardennes campaign. In early February, the Panzer divisions averaged only about 30 operational tanks each. The lack of spare parts made repair difficult if not impossible. In reality, the Panzer

A knocked-out PzKpfw IV Ausf. J, probably from 21.Panzer-Division, in the ruins of Hatten, following the January 1945 Alsace fighting. This tank was completed in November 1944 as it still retains the vision port on the turret front, dropped in November 1944, but has the gas-detection panels fitted, a November 1944 feature. The 21.Pz.Div. received 12 of these in November–December 1944.

and Panzergrenadier divisions had become infantry divisions with modest tank support. They remained a vital element for German operations, since they were generally stronger in Panzergrenadier troops than the German infantry and Volksgrenadier divisions.

The Panzer situation continued to deteriorate in February and March 1945 after these units were ground up while attempting to resist the renewed Allied offensives. By mid-March 1945, the Panzer and Panzergrenadier divisions under OB West had been reduced to a total of only 93 operational tanks, hardly more than a dozen per division. With little prospect for raising the strength of the Panzer divisions to the 1944 KStN levels, the General Inspector of Panzer Troops proposed two new divisional structures.

"Panzer-Division 1945" consolidated the two tank battalions of the 1944 Panzer regiment into a single battalion. Authorized tank strength fell from 165 to 54 tanks. Instead of remaining as a homogenous tank unit, the 1945 Panzer-Regiment would also include a Panzergrenadier-Bataillon

A Panzer IV/70(V), knocked out on the Cologne plains during fighting with the 3rd Armored Division in March 1945. The lead road wheel is the resilient steel type to compensate for the nose-heavy layout of the vehicle.

(*gepanzerte*) with the infantry riding armored half-tracks. The division's two Panzergrenadier regiments were to be converted into motorized infantry regiments without half-tracks. As a result, the 1945 division was only authorized to have 90 armored half-tracks compared to 288 in the 1944 division. Few if any of the OB West divisions underwent this reorganization for lack of time or equipment.

One of three Panther Ausf. G tanks, possibly from 9.Panzer-Division, knocked out by an M10 3in GMC of the 634th Tank Destroyer Battalion in Fernegierscheid, east of Bonn, on March 25, 1945. The tank's tactical number, possibly "812," was painted on the spare tracks on the side of the turret in white.

On April 1, the General Inspector of the Panzer Troops authorized yet another KStN to reorganize Panzer divisions that were too weak to meet the destitute Panzer-Division 1945 authorizations. The new "Kampfgruppe/Panzer-Division 1945" had an authorized strength of 8,602 men, 54 tanks, 22 Jagdpanzer tank destroyers, and 90 armored half-tracks. None of the decimated Panzer formations in the West could meet even these skeletal standards. As a result, Panzer and Panzergrenadier divisions in the final months of the war used the usual practice of combining the remnants of available combat formations into improvised *Kampfgruppen* (battle groups).

An example of this practice took place in the heavily contested Roer sector immediately after the Ardennes offensive in February 1945. Heeresgruppe B combined the battered left-overs of the 5.Panzer-Armee units from the Ardennes fighting into Korpsgruppe Bayerlein, led by the former commander of Panzer-Lehr Division, Gen. Fritz Bayerlein. The principal components were 9.Panzer-Division and 11.Panzer-Division, with the attached Tigers of s.Panzer-Abteilung.506 and s.Pz.Abt.(FKL.301) as well as the assault guns of StuG-Brigade.341. Although nominally a corps, the formation had only 130 operational tanks and AFVs, less than the authorized strength of a 1944 Panzer Division.

Korpsgruppe Bayerlein operational tank strength, Feb 1, 1945						
	PzKpfw IV	Pz.IV/70	Panther	Tiger I	Tiger II	StuG
9.Pz.Div.	6	10	5			5
11.Pz.Div.	10		32			7
s.Pz.Abt.506					18	
StuG.Bde.341						18
s.Pz.Abt.FKL.301			19			

The new Panzer brigades formed in the summer of 1944 were mostly disbanded by late 1944 due to their dismal performance in the September 1944 Lorraine offensive against Patton's Third US Army. The sole exception was Panzer-Brigade.106 "Feldherrnhalle" which was probably spared disbandment due to its Nazi-Party ties. In March 1945 the brigade was decimated in the fighting for Cologne.

The last major Panzer division deployed in the West was Panzer Division von Clausewitz. This was created from the Panzer training school at Putlos, using the remains of the decimated Panzer-Brigade.106, and elements of the

A pair of StuG III Ausf. G of StuG-Brigade.280 after the surrender in the Netherlands in May 1945. The nearest StuG III Ausf G has 16 kills marked on its barrel and the names "Mitzi" and "Erika" on the bow, while the vehicle "223" has 18 kills shown. The brigade was unusual in that two of its batteries had been reequipped with old StuG IIIs fitted with the short L/24 gun, as seen on the far left; a PzKpfw III Ausf. N is visible on the rear left. (LAC PA-168903)

embryonic 233.Ersatz-Panzer-Division from Denmark. In early April 1945, the division had at least 47 tanks and over a dozen assault guns; many of the tanks were obsolete or experimental types used at Putlos for training. For example, it still had some old Panther Ausf. D tanks. It was rushed to the Elbe front in mid-April near the junction of the 12th and 21st Army Groups between Wittenberg and Tangermünde, and so fought against both British and American units. Hastily organized and poorly trained, it was quickly decimated.

Only two Tiger units remained in the West after the transfer of 6.SS-Panzer-Armee to the East. s.Pz.Abt.506 was equipped mainly with Tiger II heavy tanks. This unit had fought in the Roer in the autumn of 1944 and again in the Ardennes offensive. Its performance in the Ardennes was so lackluster that its commander was sacked.

Schwere-Panzer-Abteilung (Fkl).301 was a specialized unit using radio-equipped Tiger I tanks to control Borgward B.IV remote control demolition vehicles. The B.IV were last used on a small scale in the Roer fighting prior to the Ardennes offensive. The unit recommended retiring these troublesome vehicles and converting the battalion to a conventional tank unit. The battalion still had some Borgward demolition vehicles when sent back into combat at the start of Operation *Lumberjack* in late February 1945, but they were seldom used.

A number of improvised Tiger units were committed in the West in 1945. The most significant of these was Panzer-Brigade Westfalen. This was activated as SS-Panzer-Ersatz Brigade Westfalen on March 29 using troops from the Waffen-SS panzer and panzer reconnaissance schools at Sennelager, north of Paderborn. The brigade consisted of two improvised infantry regiments raised from the training staff and students, with a single tank company using 15 old training tanks such as PzKpfw III. Sennelager was also

 A

1.PANTHER AUSF. G, 5./II./PZ.LEHR RGT.130, PANZER-LEHR DIVISION, GINSTERHAHN, MARCH 1945

In early 1943, the Wehrmacht adopted the practice of factory painting tanks and AFVs in overall Dark Yellow RAL 7028, and provided units with olive green RAL 6003 and red-brown 8017 to apply camouflage according to local requirements. This led to considerable variation in the field. In the summer of 1944, camouflage painting was sometimes undertaken by depots before tanks were issued to units in the hopes of conserving paint and providing more satisfactory camouflage. In August and September 1944, the camouflage was factory applied. Certain styles became predominant at the factories, and this particular tank appears to be from the MNH plant from the October to November 1944 period, judging from the pattern. The tactical vehicle number is a simple white stenciled number outline.

2.PANTHER AUSF. G, PANZER-REGIMENT.15, 11.PANZER DIVISION, SALZBURG, GERMANY, MAY 1945.

German tank plants were ordered to begin various measures to economize on paint in late 1944, including a September 1944 plan to use the basic red lead primer as the base color with sparing use of dark yellow and olive green for camouflage. In late December 1944, plans were underway to shift to a base coat of olive green with a hard-edged pattern of red-brown, though this does not appear to have been implemented until the last month of the war. This particular tank appears to have been one of the last Panthers issued to the 11. Panzer-Division.

1

2

A Jagdpanzer 38 of Panzerjäger-Abteilung.257 knocked out during fighting with the 142nd Infantry, 36th Division in Oberhoffen-sur-Moder in Alsace. On February 11, 1945, the 257. Volksgrenadier-Division staged a counterattack, including three of its thirteen Jagdpanzer 38s, two of which were knocked out by bazooka fire. This one has suffered a catastrophic ammunition fire, which has ripped open the right-side armor.

the location for reequipping army tank battalions with the new Tiger II heavy tank, which was manufactured in nearby Kassel. At the time, s.Pz. Abt. 507 was at Sennelager to replenish after its heavy losses on the Russian front. It had 21 Tiger II tanks and 3 Jagdpanthers on hand at the end of March and these were attached to the renamed Panzer-Brigade Westfalen. This unit fought against the US Army's 3rd Armored Division around Paderborn in early April 1945, and was burned out in the process.

There were less than a dozen Panzerjäger-Abteilungen (tank destroyer battalions) under OB West in 1945; these amounted to about a quarter of its armored strength. Five of these were equipped with a variety of types armed with 7.5cm guns, including the Panzer IV/70 (formerly Jagdpanzer IV). Three others, s.Pz.Jg.Abt. 519, 654, and 655, were equipped with the Jagdpanther. The sole operational Jagdtiger battalion, s.Pz.Jg.Abt.653, also served in the West. There were two company-strength Nashorn units in the West in 1945, 1./s.Pz.Jg.Abt.93 and 1./s.Pz.Jg.Abt.525, as well as Nashorns in other Panzerjäger units such as s.Pz.Jg.Abt.654.

Sturmgeschütz-Brigaden (assault gun brigades) were relatively uncommon in the West compared to the East. There were only seven of these in OB West in February 1945. Contrary to their name, they were in fact battalion-sized with an average strength of only 20 vehicles. They were generally assigned to infantry corps to provide infantry close support. These battalions were generally equipped with the StuG.III and StuG.IV rather than the substitute Jagdpanzer 38.

Infantry and Volksgrenadier divisions had an organic Panzerjäger-Battaillon that could include a towed and a self-propelled 7.5cm company. By 1945, most infantry and Volksgrenadier self-propelled gun companies substituted the new Jagdpanzer 38 for the StuG III. In February 1945, OB West had self-propelled gun companies in 36 of its infantry and Volksgrenadier divisions. About a third of the divisions were armed only with Panzerschreck rocket launchers and towed antitank guns.

There was only a single assault howitzer battalion in the West, Sturm-Panzer-Abteilung.217, equipped with the 15cm Stumpanzer IV. One of the most obscure Panzer units was Panzer-Flamm-Kompanie.352, which fought in Alsace at the time of Operation *Nordwind*. It was equipped with a flamethrower version of the Jagdpanzer 38. Rounding out the menagerie of oddities were three assault mortar companies, Sturm-Mörser-Kompanien.1000–1002, each equipped with four Sturmtigers.

OB West Panzer strength by unit type, February 5, 1945						
	Panzer & Pz.Gren. Div.	Panzerjäger Abt.	Stug. Brigade	Inf. Div.	Total	Operational
Pz.III/IV	68+42				110	68
Panther	96+123				219	96
Tiger	26+35				61	26
7.5cm Sfl	48+53				101	48
Jagdpanther		43+23			66	43
Jagdtiger		21+7			28	21
Nashorn		8+4			12	8
Stug/Jagdpanzer	113+113	168+140	101+52	212+141	1,040	594
Stu.Panzer	15+17				32	15
Operational	**366**	**240**	**101**	**212**		**919**
Total	**749**	**414**	**153**	**353**	**1,669**	
*Operational + In repair/combat damaged						

US Army

Of the sixteen armored divisions raised by the US Army in World War II, all but one were deployed to the ETO (European Theater of Operations); 1st Armored Division remained in Italy until the end of the war. With two exceptions, the armored divisions in the ETO were in the "light" 1943 TO&E (table of organization and equipment). These divisions contained a balanced mix of three tank battalions, three armored infantry battalions, and three armored field artillery battalions.

The other two divisions, the 2nd and 3rd Armored Divisions, retained the earlier "heavy" 1942 TO&E. This configuration had two armored regiments with three tank battalions each but only a single armored infantry regiment with three battalions. This resulted in a tank-heavy configuration with six tank battalions and three armored infantry battalions. The reasons for this exception were bureaucratic rather than doctrinal. During the conversion of the divisions from the 1942 to 1943 pattern, Lt Gen. Jacob Devers was head of the US Army in the ETO. Devers had previously led the Armored Force and he did not agree with the Army Ground Forces rationale for the new 1943 organization. He argued that it was too disruptive to convert the two divisions already in Britain, the 2nd and 3rd Armored Divisions, to the 1943

An M4A1 Duplex Drive (DD) amphibious tank of the 748th Tank Battalion enters the water during the Rhine crossing operations by Patton's Third US Army near Nierstein on March 23, 1945. The canvas skirt has been erected around the tank and the twin propellors are visible at the rear.

An M5A1 light tank of Co. D, 761st Tank Battalion (Colored) in front of the statue of Prince Albert in Coburg market square on April 11, 1945. This was one of two segregated African-American tank battalions in the US 12th Army Group.

pattern. As a result, the 2nd and 3rd Armored Divisions retained a modified version of the 1942 pattern.

In practice, the unbalanced configuration of the heavy armored divisions proved to be a problem, since there was too little infantry for many operations. The solution was to attach an infantry regiment from a neighboring infantry division for significant operations. This essentially created a mini-armored corps.

These two divisions played a vital role in two of the most important operations of the war, the Ardennes offensive and the encirclement of the Ruhr. In the Ardennes, the 2nd Armored Division encircled the lead elements of 5.Panzer-Armee in the Celles pocket outside Bastogne, ending the German advance. The 3rd Armored Division counterattacked the II.SS-Panzer-Korps on the approaches to the Tailles plateau, preventing a breakthrough in that sector. During the Ruhr encirclement, these two divisions were the pincers of Bradley's 12th Army Group envelopment of Heeregruppe B. The 2nd Armored Division was the spearhead of the Ninth US Army on the northern side of the Ruhr pocket, and the 3rd Armored Division was the spearhead of the First US Army on the southern side.

The core tenet of US Army armored doctrine was the combined arms team, a practice borrowed from the study of the German Blitzkrieg-era Panzer division. Each 1943-pattern armored division had three Combat Command headquarters (CCA, CCB, CCR/Reserve). The combat command was a temporary brigade, tailored to the mission. Typically, each combat command would have a tank battalion, an armored infantry battalion, and an armored field artillery battalion, plus companies from other elements such as armored engineer, tank destroyers, and anti-aircraft artillery. The

B

1. M4A3E2 ASSAULT TANK, 69TH TANK BATTALION, 6TH ARMORED DIVISION, GERMANY, MARCH 1945

The 6th Armored Division was one of the few US armored divisions to regularly use battalion markings on their tanks. The 69th "Black Panther" Tank Battalion sometimes painted a stalking black panther in the stars on their tanks during the spring of 1945, as seen here. The 15th "Wolf-Pack" Tank Battalion used a gray wolf-head insignia (inset (i)) on top of the Armored Force triangle, while the 68th Tank Battalion used the "Toby Tortoise" cartoon (inset (ii)) and/or a white triangle. The other markings are typical of the 6th Armored Division, including the large speed numbers on the hull side to facilitate radio communication between the tanks.

2. M4A3 (76MM) 2EME SECTION, 1ÈRE COMPAGNIE, 501E RCC (RÉGIMENT DE CHARS DE COMBAT), 2E DIVISION BLINDÉE, ALSACE, 1945

The tanks of the 2eme Section, 1ère Compagnie generally named their tanks after Tunisian towns based on the unit's combat in the area in 1943. *Médenine II* was the second tank to bear this name. The first, a 75mm M4A2, was knocked out in August 1944. The 501e RCC generally painted their tank names on the hull side in green with white trim. On the gun barrel is the name "Le Râleur" (*The Grouch*). The divisional insignia, a map of France with the superimposed Cross of Lorraine, was usually painted on the hull side along with the French flag to the rear.

(i)

(ii)

1

"LE RÂLEUR"

MEDENINE II

2

A pair of M24s of Company D, 736th Tank Battalion come ashore from LCM (landing craft mechanized) during the Saale river crossings on April 16, 1945 while supporting the 83rd Division, Ninth US Army. By this time, this battalion had completely replaced its older M5A1 light tanks with the new M24.

combat commands could have other compositions for specific missions, for example two armored infantry battalions for some missions, such as fighting in urban areas or forests. The combined-arms composition of the combat commands was carried a step further at company level with the temporary organization of task forces within the combat command. These consisted of several mixed companies from the combat command's attached battalions.

Of the 88 US Army tank battalions deployed to the ETO, 51 were organic to the armored divisions while 37 were separate tank battalions. The separate tank battalions were primarily used for support of the infantry divisions. The original pattern in the summer of 1944 was to deploy an armored group headquarters with each corps. These had two or three separate tank battalions attached. The armored group headquarters could then deploy its tank battalions en masse as a concentrated armored force, or dole out the tank battalions to the infantry battalions for support. This doctrine was largely ignored in the ETO, as the corps commanders had recognized since the 1943 Tunisian campaign that infantry divisions regularly needed tank support in the conduct of offensive operations. There were never enough separate tank battalions to permanently incorporate a tank battalion in each infantry division. Instead, tank battalions were assigned to infantry divisions on a temporary basis, depending on their mission. Since their tactical role had almost entirely evaporated, in late October 1944 the armored group staffs were gradually reassigned as CCR headquarters in the armored divisions.

One separate tank battalion, the 759th, was configured in the unusual light tank configuration, equipped only with M5A1 light tanks. Three tank battalions were nominally under the special mine exploder configuration, the 738th, 739th, and 740th Tank Battalions (SMX). The plan was to deploy one SMX battalion per field army as an equivalent of the Armoured Funnies of the British 79th Armoured Division. In the event, the 738th Tank Battalion (SMX) became part of the First US Army and the 739th Tank Battalion (SMX) was attached to Ninth US Army. The 740th Tank Battalion was still awaiting equipment at the time of the Ardennes campaign and was hastily rushed to Belgium as part of the reinforcement effort. It never received specialized equipment, and so reverted to the standard 1943 tank battalion TO&E.

A total of 55 tank destroyer battalions were deployed to the ETO. Of these, 15 were attached to the armored divisions. The remainder was deployed at corps level under a tank destroyer group headquarters. As in the case of the separate tank battalions, the tank destroyer battalions were generally attached to infantry divisions for fire support. There were two different configurations of these battalions – self-propelled and towed. The Army Ground Forces had begun converting 15 self-propelled battalions to towed battalions in 1943, based on a mistaken interpretation of the combat lessons of the Tunisian campaign. During the fighting in France in 1944, the towed battalions had demonstrated inferior combat effectiveness to the self-propelled battalions. The continued poor performance of the towed battalions in the Ardennes campaign was the last straw, and the towed battalions were largely converted to self-propelled ones during 1945.

Of the various armored formations of the US Army, the tank destroyer battalions were the most problematic. They had been designed to counter the massed Panzer attacks of the 1940–41 Blitzkrieg era, and so they were primarily defensive in orientation. This doctrinal orientation was ill-suited to the offensive posture of the US Army in the ETO. Facing so few Panzers in 1945, tank destroyers ended up being used as surrogate tanks for direct fire support of the infantry.

The US Army's cavalry regiments were reorganized in late 1943 and 1944 as CRSM (cavalry reconnaissance squadrons-mechanized). The CRSM were mixed armored car/tank units with 40 M8 light armored cars, 17 M5A1 light tanks, 6 M8 75mm howitzer motor carriages, and 30 half-tracks. The CRSM in the ETO were deployed as organic elements of the armored divisions or subordinated to cavalry group headquarters. They conducted the traditional cavalry roles of scouting and flank security. A total of thirteen cavalry groups served in the ETO in 1944–45.

Besides the 15 US armored divisions, the French Army deployed three armored divisions that had been raised and trained by the US Army. For political reasons, the 2e Division Blindée usually served under US command, while the 1er and 5e Divisions Blindées served in the 1er Armée Française (First French Army). The French divisions were all organized under the standard US Army 1943 TO&E, although the battalions retained traditional French regimental designations.

A pair of French M10 3in GMCs of the 2e Escadron, 11e Regiment de Chasseurs d'Afrique of the 5e Division Blindée supporting infantry of the 1re Armée Française near the German Rhine bridgehead at Gambsheim in Alsace on February 9, 1945. The crew has mounted a captured German MG 34 machine gun on the turret of the tank destroyer in the foreground.

The Sherman V formed the backbone of the tank units of Montgomery's 21st Army Group. These tanks are from the Governor General's Foot Guards, Canadian 4th Armoured Division in Sonsbeck during Operation *Blockbuster*, the fighting in the Hochwald west of the Rhine on March 9, 1945.

British/Canadian Armies

Montgomery's 21st Army Group included six standard armoured divisions: three British divisions (7th, 11th, and Guards), two Canadian (4th and 5th) and one Polish division (1st). These were organized in the same fashion, based around an armoured brigade, an infantry brigade, and divisional troops. Each armoured brigade generally had three armoured regiments, an armoured reconnaissance regiment and a motor (infantry) battalion. The division's infantry brigade had three lorried infantry battalions. Divisional

The best British tank in 1945 was the new Comet, a further evolution of the Cromwell armed with the new 77mm gun. This Comet of the 29th Armoured Brigade, 11th Armoured Division is seen passing through a town northwest of the Rhine crossing point at Wesel on March 30, 1945.

troops included two field artillery regiments (one towed, one SP) and an armoured reconnaissance regiment.

Besides these standard divisions, the 79th Armoured Division was used to manage regiments operating the "Armoured Funnies." These were specialized tanks including counter-obstacle tanks such as the Churchill AVRE, mine-clearing tanks such as the Crab flail tanks, and flamethrower tanks such as the Churchill Crocodile. This division did not operate as a unified formation, but was rather an administrative headquarters that distributed its component formations to support other units of 21st Army Group.

Besides the seven armored divisions, the 21st Army Group had eleven armored/tank brigades subordinated to the corps of the Second British Army and First Canadian Army. They were used to provide armored support to the corps' infantry divisions. Of these brigades, two were Canadian and one was Czech. The tank brigades were the original infantry-support formations, equipped with Churchill infantry tanks. The independent armored brigades were created when the armored divisions shed a brigade during reorganization in 1942–43. They were equipped with cruiser tanks such as the Sherman. Montgomery's preference for a "universal tank" rather than the old distinction of infantry/cruiser tanks led to a unification of the designation, with the tank brigades being redesignated as armored brigades in February 1945. Of the brigades, three were based around the Churchill infantry tank, while most of the

1. VALENTINE 17PDR, 102ND ANTI-TANK REGIMENT, 15TH SCOTTISH DIVISION, GERMANY, APRIL 1945

The 102nd Anti-Tank Regiment served with the 15th Scottish Division in 1945. In early March 1945, A Battery's two-towed 6pdr troops were converted to Valentine 17pdrs, making it totally self-propelled. The B, C, and D Batteries traded their 6pdrs for towed 17pdrs, so each of these batteries had one troop of Valentine 17pdrs and two towed troops. The Valentine 17pdrs carried the usual unit markings on the hull front and rear, the "46" on a Royal Artillery red/blue square identifying the regiment, and the 15th Division insignia opposite. The tactical sign in the center would normally have been a blue square with a smaller red square, with the location of the smaller square indicating the battery. However, this unit painted the marking in Yeomanry colors of light and dark blue instead of the usual Royal Artillery blue/red. The "LI" indicated the troop/gun number. A small Allied star was painted on the superstructure side. The vehicle census number (eg. S279543) was carried on the corner superstructure panels towards the front of the vehicle, not evident in this view. The vehicle was finished in overall SCC 15 olive drab.

2. COMET, 3 RTR, 29TH ARMOURED BRIGADE, 11TH ARMOURED DIVISION, GERMANY APRIL 1945

In April 1944, the British Army released ACI 533/44 which adopted SCC 15 (Standard Camouflage Colour 15) olive drab as the standard color for army equipment. The aim was to avoid the need to repaint Lend–Lease American equipment such as tanks. As a result, the Comet shown here was finished in SCC 15. The markings are in the usual fashion with the 52 on a red square identifying the regiment with the divisional insignia, the Black Bull on the opposite side. The vehicle name, CRUSADER, is in the center. The tactical insignia would be repeated on the rear of the tank as well.

1

2

remainder used the Sherman tank. The Czech Armoured Brigade was an outlier, based on the Cromwell tank.

The accompanying chart shows the growth of the armored holdings of the 21st Army Group from January to May 1945. The "unit" column includes the unit holdings of tanks and AFVs. The "other" category includes tanks and AFVs in reserve including vehicle parks, in transit, in replacement and training units, and under repair outside the combat units.

21st Army Group tank/AFV strength						
	27 Jan 45			**5 May 45**		
	Unit	Other	Sub-total	Unit	Other	Sub-total
Churchill	725	688	1,413	744	587	1,331
Valentine	85	199	284	295	161	456
Sherman	2,130	1,570	3,700	2,383	1,730	4,113
M10	240	172	412	292	125	417
Cromwell	771	375	1,146	885	579	1,464
Stuart	446	344	790	601	304	905
Locust	0	0	0	9	88	97
Chaffee	0	0	0	22	66	88
Total	**4,397**	**3,348**	**7,745**	**5,231**	**3,640**	**8,871**

TECHNICAL FACTORS

Wehrmacht

The technical composition of the Panzerwaffe during the final campaign in Germany in 1945 was essentially similar to the Ardennes campaign, except for the far more battered condition of most Panzer units.[1] The Panzerwaffe continued to decline in both quantity and quality. At the end of the Ardennes campaign, about 59 percent of tanks and AFVs in OB West were operational, the remainder being battle damaged or under mechanical repair. The operational fraction of the tank inventory shrunk to 55 percent by February 5, 1945 and only 40 percent on March 15.

---

1   Steven Zaloga, *Tanks in the Battle of the Bulge*, Osprey New Vanguard 281 (2018).

The backbone of the tank force remained the PzKpfw IV and its derivatives. Production of the PzKpfw IV Ausf. H ended at Vomag and Krupp in July 1944, and the subsequent PzKpfw IV Ausf. J was manufactured only at the Nibelungenwerke until March 1945, when it ceased altogether. As a result, the proportion of PzKpfw IV tanks declined steadily in 1945. At the start of the Ardennes offensive, the PzKpfw IV represented 41 percent of the tank force. This fell to only 28 percent by February 5, and only 25 percent by March 15.

Ideally, the Wehrmacht would have liked to up-gun the PzKpfw IV Ausf. J with the longer PaK 42 L/70 gun used in the Panther. However, this was not practical due to the recoil limits of its smaller turret ring. However, it was possible to mount the L/70 gun in the tank destroyer version of the PzKpfw IV, the Jagdpanzer IV. When this upgrade entered production in August 1944, it was redesignated as the Panzer IV/70 to indicate that it could be used as a tank substitute. The original version, manufactured by Vomag, was designated as the Panzer IV/70 (V). Nibelungenwerke also manufactured a comparable version but with a higher superstructure, named the Panzer IV/70 (A).

The Panzer IV/70 had a number of advantages over the basic tank version, including the more powerful PaK 42 L/70 gun and better frontal armor. However, the gun was mounted in a fixed casemate, making the vehicle less effective in close-combat due to the limited traverse of the gun. The main problem with the vehicle was that the long gun barrel was a significant hindrance when driving cross-country, especially in the Vomag version with its very low superstructure. The gun barrel could easily be slammed into the ground if the vehicle moved into a depression. The forward-mounted gun and heavy glacis armor also created greater stress on the front of the suspension. The vehicle's side armor was mediocre, and the location of ammunition on the casemate side walls made the vehicle prone to catastrophic ammunition fires when hit on the sides. Nevertheless, the Panzer IV/70 was a formidable tank killer when employed from ambush position, a circumstance which was relatively common during the final months of the war.

A PzKpfw IV Ausf. J number 223 of 2./Panzer-Regiment.33, 9.Panzer-Division, one of three knocked out on February 27, 1945, by the T26E3 Pershing tank of Sgt Nicholas Mashlonik of Co. E, 33rd Armored, 3rd Armored Division on the outskirts of the town of Elsdorf. Panzer-Regiment.33 was named after Prinz Eugen and so carried the insignia of a knight on a charging horse, visible immediately on the front of the turret skirt.

A Panzer IV/70 (A), possibly from StuG.Brigade.341, knocked out in March 1945 during fighting with the US 78th Division in the grounds of Haus Neuglück near Bennerscheid, Germany, possibly by the 745th Tank Battalion. This version of the Panzer IV/70 had a higher superstructure than the type produced at Vomag. The four front roadwheels here are the resilient steel type, instead of the normal rubber rimmed type, used to accommodate the higher weight load on the front of the chassis.

By the time of the Ardennes offensive, the Panther had become the single most common German tank type. The percentage of Panthers in the Panzerwaffe in the West increased due to the decline of PzKpfw IV production. On January 15, 1945 the Panthers accounted for 39 percent of the total, 56 percent on February 5, and 63 percent on March 15, not counting the Panzer IV/70 in the final tally. At the same time, it should be noted that the Panzerwaffe in the West was shrinking catastrophically with only 49 operational Panthers on the whole front on March 15, declining to only 24 on April 10. The Panther was still a formidable rival to any Allied tank, but it was available in such puny numbers, thus it was rarely a threat after January 1945. It continued to be plagued by mechanical problems, especially its weak final drive. For example, of 152 Panthers in OB West's hands on March 15, only 49 (32 percent) were operational. This was due to the declining quality of German manufacturing, which was exacerbated by the poor training of new drivers, as well as a chronic shortage of spare parts.

The Tiger saw combat in very small numbers in 1945, though its importance has been greatly exaggerated due to the tendency of Allied tank crews to refer to any German AFV they encountered as a Tiger. To put this in some perspective, there were only twenty-six operational in the West on February 5, six on March 15, and ten on April 10. Only two regular units in the West still operated the Tiger, s.Pz.Abt.(FKL).301 using the older Tiger I, and s.Pz.Abt.506 using the Tiger II. Due to the presence of the Tiger manufacturing plant at Kassel and a nearby Tiger training facility, there was an upsurge in improvised Tiger II deployment in March 1945 during the fighting for the Ruhr pocket. This involved hastily formed units such as Panzer Brigade Westfalen, which was mentioned earlier, as well as smaller improvised units, hastily thrown into action with Tiger tanks.

There was a small number of other tank types that saw combat in Germany in 1945. The PzKpfw III was operational in modest numbers, though most serving under OB West were the Beobachtungs artillery observer tanks. The last regions in which the normal tank version was in widespread use were in peripheral theaters such as Norway and Denmark. A number of obsolete and captured types saw combat in 1945, usually in desperate last-ditch stands by training units.

The StuG III, like the PzKpfw IV, was a declining presence in the Wehrmacht due to reduced production. A low-cost substitute, the "Sturmgeschütz neuer Art," was developed, based on a modified Czech PzKpfw 38(t) chassis. It entered production in April 1944 as the Jagdpanzer 38. The change in designation was largely due to the influence of the General Inspector of Panzer Troops, Heinz Guderian, who became army chief of staff in July 1944. Guderian had long been an opponent of the Sturmgeschütz, complaining that it took away precious industrial resources from his favored Panzerwaffe. In the event, the

The PzKpfw III was uncommon in the West in 1945 except in peripheral theaters such as Norway. This is the surrender of Panzer-Brigade Norwegen at Trandum, Norway to British officers in May 1945. Most of the tanks here are the final PzKpfw III Ausf. N version. There were 68 PzKpfw IIIs in service in Norway in 1945.

Jagdpanzer 38 was used primarily in the Panzerjäger battalions of the infantry and Volksgrenadier divisions as a substitute for the StuG III assault gun. In contrast, the dedicated StuG brigades were generally supplied from the existing inventory of StuG III and StuG IV assault guns. Dedicated Panzerjäger battalions tended to use the Panzer IV/70 or heavier types.

The Jagdpanzer 38 was significantly inferior to the StuG III. Although it had good frontal armor, the side armor was only proof against small arms fire.

The crew compartment was an ergonomic mess that was excessively cramped. The commander had a hard time controlling the vehicle due to his awkward location and completely inadequate vision devices. Its main advantage was that it was relatively cheap to produce at the two plants in the Czech provinces that were not ready to manufacture larger and heavier armored vehicles. This vehicle was sometimes called the Hetzer by German troops, though this was not its official designation.

There were a number of other types of 7.5cm Panzerjägers in service in 1945. Most of the self-propelled Marder III 7.5cm PaK 40 had disappeared from production in early 1944 in favor of the Jagdpanzer 38, and the inventory of these vehicles had largely been exhausted in 1944 through combat attrition. The self-propelled version of the 7.5cm PaK 40 on the RSO tractor was not widely used in the West, though it was occasionally encountered in Germany. The Sd.Kfz.251/22 armored half-track with the 7.5cm PaK 40 was deployed on a small scale in the Panzergrenadier regiments.

Three heavier Panzerjägers were in service in 1945. The 8.8cm Pak 43/1 Nashorn, based on the PzKpfw III/IV chassis, was in use in the West in 1945 in very small numbers. It mounted a very potent gun, but was very lightly armored with an open top. It was intended primarily for long-range ambush engagements.

The best of the Panzerjäger designs was the Jagdpanther, which combined the Panther chassis with the same powerful 8.8cm gun as the Tiger II. It had excellent frontal armor as well, making it a formidable tank destroyer. However, it suffered the same flaws in its power train as the basic Panther. This was exacerbated by the excessive weight towards the front of the vehicle and the difficulty of repairing the transmission and frontal drive in the field. Although three Jagdpanther battalions were deployed in the West, the number of operational vehicles at any one time was usually small due both to a shortage of new vehicles, and mechanical problems. On April 10, 1944, OB West had 30 of these, of which 5 were functional and 22 under repair; the rest were presumably in transit.

The heaviest and most powerful armored vehicle in service in World War II was the 12.8cm Jagdtiger, based on the Tiger II chassis. For inexplicable reasons, the units equipped with this gargantuan vehicle were deployed in the West rather than on the Russian front. The 12.8cm gun was grossly excessive for any Allied tank it faced in the West; it

One of the more obscure German AFVs was the Flammpanzer 38, a flamethrower derivative of the Jagdpanzer 38 tank destroyer, fitted with a *Köbe Flammenwerfer* instead of a gun. This vehicle was ordered specifically by Hitler for use in the Nordwind offensive in Alsace in early 1945, and it was used by Panzer-Flamm-Kompanie.352 in support of the 25.Panzergrenadier-Division in the assault on Hatten-Ritterhofen in early January 1945.

made somewhat more sense in the East, where it would have faced the heavily armored IS-2 and ISU-152. The relatively short combat ranges that were typical along Germany's industrialized western frontier obviated the need for its long-range performance. It was awkward to employ in a mobile fashion, since few bridges were strong enough to accommodate a 70-ton monster. On April 10, 1945, OB West had 55 on hand, of which 24 were operational and 15 under repair; the others were presumably in transit. They did not see very much combat.

Eighteen old Tiger I tanks were converted into 38cm Sturmmörser Tigers, with a RW61 breech-loaded mortar fitted into a new fixed casemate. This example was commanded by Lt Doll from Stu.Mrs.Kp. 1001. It was immobilized on April 10 due to track problems, and was captured after a short skirmish with the US 1/13th Infantry, 8th Division in Hützemert, east of Cologne.

The oddest Tiger variant in use in the West was the 38cm Sturmmörser, sometimes called the Sturmtiger. This was a conversion of an older Tiger I chassis with a fixed casemate replacing the turret. It was fitted with a breech-loaded, 38cm rocket-assisted mortar. This type was first used in combat to crush the Warsaw uprising in August 1944. They were used in attempts to knock down the Remagen bridge, but their combat record was inconsequential.

A technical comparison of the Panzers to their Allied equivalents is impossible in the limited space available here. After the war, the British army attempted to assess the relative technical effectiveness of German and British tanks. However, it did not consider factors such as training, crew experience, or battlefield circumstances. The results are summarized on the accompanying chart. The numerical rating indicates the effectiveness ratio of the specified German tank vs. the specified British tank with a rating of 1.0 indicating they were equivalent. So in the first case of the PzKpfw IV Ausf H in a duel at 1,000yds, it was 1.35 times more effective than the Cromwell but only 90 percent as effective as a Sherman Firefly.

1 JAGDPANTHER, 1/S.PZ.JG.ABT. 654, GERMANY, MARCH 1945

This Jagdpanther is in the typical post-September 1944 scheme of red lead primer with patches of RAL 7028 dark yellow and RAL 6003 olive green. This unit had the practice of removing the tool stowage from the sides of the vehicle and rearranging them on the rear for more convenient access, a process that was undertaken when the unit was reequipping at Grafenwohr in October 1944. As a result, the outlines of the tool racks can be seen silhouetted on the hull side where the red lead primer has been exposed.

2 TIGER II, S.PZ.ABT. 507, PANZERGRUPPE HUDEL, GERMANY, APRIL 1945

This Tiger II was one of a number provided to s.PzAbt. 507 before the unit was hastily dispatched towards Remagen as part of the improvised Panzergruppe Hudel, intended to crush the US bridgehead after the capture of the Ludendorff bridge. It is finished in the late factory scheme of overall RAL 6003 olive green with small bands of RAL 7028 dark yellow. The edges of both colors have small splotches of the opposite color to break up the pattern, a relatively late example of "ambush" camouflage. The unit did not have time to apply tactical markings and photos of their tanks from this period show no tactical numbers.

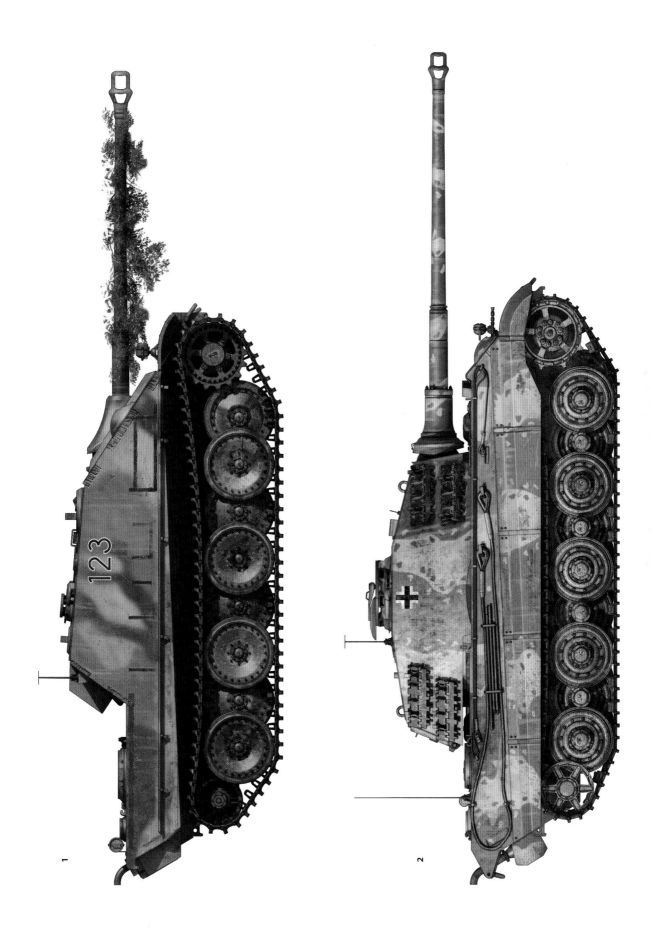

1

2

German vs. British tank combat effectiveness					
	Range (yards)	Cromwell	Sherman 75mm	Sherman 17 pdr
PzKpfw IV Ausf. H	1,000	1.35	1.1	0.9
	1,500	1.5	0.9	
Panther Ausf G	300	1.85	1.55	1.2
	600	1.85	1.55	1.2
	1,000		2.0	
Tiger I	300	1.9	1.65	
	600	1.9	1.6	0.9
	1,000			0.9
Kingtiger	300	3.2	2.7	
	600	3.2	2.7	1.55
	1,000			1.75

E. Benn, R. Shephard, *Tank Effectiveness: A Comparison of the Theoretical Measure with Observed Battle Performance* (AORG Report No. 6/52, 1952)

US Army

The backbone of the US Army tank force was the M4 medium tank in its many variants. After the numerous tank engagements in the Ardennes campaign, tank units wanted more of the 76mm versions. As a result, ETOUSA requested that future shipments of tanks to the ETO favor the 76mm gun tanks over the 75mm tanks. There was a slight discrepancy in the delivery of the 76mm tank between the armored divisions and the separate tank battalions. As can be seen in the accompanying chart, the 76mm tanks did not become the majority until the very end of the war in May 1945.

12th Army Group medium tank strength 1945: *(75mm gun vs. 76mm gun)**					
Armored Division	Jan	Feb	Mar	Apr	May
2	117+21	143+66	143+65	143+87	95+95
3	138+40	155+44	143+51	119+40	86+90
4	68+16	112+42	91+49	48+68	54+105
5	127+10	123+35	114+35	106+66	77+62
6	139+11	66+44	87+56	45+74	30+128
7	61+36	94+41	118+50	77+61	72+80
8		107+47	116+47	80+70	77+70
9	13+95	51+116	50+116	55+97	52+96
10	85+34	84+49	86+43	84+84	66+100
11	98+44	81+58	91+61	88+61	68+74
12	109+52	93+44	78+90	84+84	86+83
13					91+70
14				83+88	65+68
16				117+51	115+49
20				117+51	0+165
Sub-total	*955+359*	*1,109+586*	*1,117+663*	*1,246+982*	*1,034+1,335*
% 76mm in AD	**27.3**	**34.5**	**37.2**	**44.0**	**56.3**
Separate tank battalions					
Sep. TB	695+259	733+216	781+305	669+438	567+607
% 76mm in TB	**27.1**	**22.7**	**28.1**	**39.5**	**51.7**
Overall	**1650+618**	**1,842+802**	**1,898+968**	**1,915+1420**	**1,601+1,942**
M4 Total	**2,268**	**2,644**	**2,866**	**3,335**	**3,543**

75mm + 76mm; data as of beginning of each month.

Since 1943, the US Army policy was to favor the M4A3 version with the Ford GAA engine over the earlier M4/M4A1 types with the Continental radial engine. The US Army in the ETO did not generally use either the M4A2 or M4A4 versions, though small numbers were transferred from British stocks in January 1945 to make up for the Ardennes tank casualties. M4 tank production in early 1944 shifted to a modified hull design that could be distinguished by larger driver/co-driver hatches. The most important aspect of this improvement

was the introduction of "wet" ammunition stowage to reduce the probability of ammunition fires if the tank armor was penetrated. These tanks had a (W) appended to their designation by the Ordnance Department, such as M4A3(W), though in practice, this awkward and non-standard designation was seldom used by the combat units of the Army Ground Forces.

Another important change introduced on the M4 series at the end of 1944 was the new HVSS (horizontal volute spring suspension) with its wider 23in track. This gave the M4 better mobility in the muddy and wet conditions. This suspension first appeared in the ETO on the M4A3 (76mm) tank, which was awkwardly referred to as the "M4A3 (76) w/23-in. track." Eventually, the designation "M4A3E8" was unofficially used, the "E8" referring to the new HVSS suspension.

ETOUSA tank and tank destroyer strength in 1945*					
	Jan	**Feb**	**Mar**	**Apr**	**May**
M5A1	2,950	3,351	2,618	2,695	3,005
M24	20	128	363	732	1,114
M8 HMC	672	680	515	485	485
M4 (75,76mm)	4,561	5,297	6,249	5,727	6,336
M4 (105)	620	804	612	612	636
T26E3	0	0	20	39	105
M18	312	448	540	427	427
M10	768	686	684	427	427
M36	365	826	684	1,054	1,029
Total	**10,268**	**12,220**	**12,285**	**12,198**	**13,564**

*as of the 20th of each month

Besides the basic M4 gun tanks, the US Army also used M4 105mm assault guns in each tank battalion. These were armed with a 105mm howitzer to provide indirect fire support. There were three of these in each tank battalion headquarters and one in each medium tank company. Some battalions combined all six into a single platoon.

The 12th Army Group also used rocket-armed tanks for the artillery role, primarily the T34 4.5in rocket launcher. Tanks of the 743rd Tank Battalion had Calliope launchers installed for a planned operation in

An M4A3E8 (76mm) of Task Force Richardson, 3rd Armored Division, moves across a treadway bridge over the Erft canal near Paffendorf on February 28, 1945 during Operation *Grenade*. This is a very early production example of the M4A3 (76mm) with the HVSS suspension, lacking the usual muzzle brake on the 76mm gun.

December 1944. However, the German attack in the Ardennes preempted this operation and the launchers were discarded without being used. The T34 was more extensively deployed in early 1945, and was used in small numbers at various times by the 2nd, 4th, 6th, 12th, and 14th Armored Divisions and by the 712th, 753rd, and 781st Tank Battalions. In general, the launchers were unpopular with tank commanders, as they felt that the artillery mission should be performed by artillery units and not tank units.

In November 1944, when the US Army first began planning future operations to cross the Rhine, there were only 118 M4A1 DDs still available, so British DDs were supplied to the US Army to make up for shortfalls. These included both the Sherman III (M4A2) and Sherman V (M4A4) DD tanks. In the event, far fewer DD tanks were used for the Rhine crossing than originally anticipated. Company C, 736th Tank Battalion with the Ninth Army crossed the Rhine on 23–24 March 1945, mostly equipped with British M4A2 DD tanks, but with a few M4A1 DD tanks as well. The 748th Tank Battalion had 51 DD tanks, but a long road march to the Rhine damaged the specialized equipment and only 18 were floatable. A total of eight were launched across the Rhine near Oppenheim on 23–24 March 1945, with one sinking. Ten more were ferried across. This was the last time that the DD tanks were used in an amphibious role during the war, though the tanks continued to serve as normal gun tanks with their skirts removed.

By 1945, US tank units were not satisfied with the armored protection offered by the M4 tank. Ordnance developmental efforts to develop armor upgrade kits were not ready before the war ended. As a result, many units employed expedients for added protection. The use of sand-bags for additional protection began in the summer of 1944, usually on a local basis. The proliferation of infantry antitank rocket launchers such as the Panzerschreck and Panzerfaust in 1945 accelerated local US countermeasures. Many of these efforts were sponsored at corps or field army level. The Ninth US Army developed a layered package consisting of spare tracks at the bottom, covered by sand bags. Patton's Third US Army explicitly forbade the use of sand-bags after their Ordnance officers declared them too heavy and ineffective. Instead, Third US Army began a program of cannibalizing knocked-out German and American tanks for their armor plate, and welding it onto their tanks. Seventh US Army in January 1945 began a systematic practice of fitting tanks with special cages that could be filled with sand bags over the front and sides. This package was sometimes augmented with layers of steel-reinforced concrete over the hull glacis plate. Some units had their own programs. For example, when 3rd Armored Division captured Cologne, they used a local steel plant to modify their tanks with additional plates of steel.

There was considerable controversy over these various upgrade programs. Many Ordnance officers felt that sand bags were insufficient to protect against antitank rockets. But most unit commanders considered the psychological benefits of the added protection to be sufficient to encourage the programs.

The ultimate solution to the armor problem was better tank armor. Only 250 M4A3E2 assault tanks were manufactured, and these were highly prized by armored divisions and separate

The new HVSS suspension was also used on late-production M4A3 (105mm) assault guns, as seen on this example from Patton's Third US Army along the Inn river on the Austrian border in May 1945.

tank battalions in the ETO. They were often used for especially hazardous missions, such as being used at the head of a column. About a hundred of these were up-gunned with 76mm guns in early 1945.

A replacement for the M4 series had been on the back-burner since 1942, and the program was accelerated in early 1944 due to the growing threat of the Panther and Tiger tanks. The first batches of T26E3 Pershing heavy tanks arrived in the ETO in February 1945. They saw limited combat service due to their small numbers.

T26E3 heavy tank strength in ETO 1945			
Division	Mar	Apr	May
2		19	21
3	10	10	18
5			17
9	10	10	17
11			32
Total	20	39	105

Due to the failure of the M7 light tank problem, the M5A1 remained the principal light tank in the US Army through 1945. A significantly improved design, the M24 Chaffee, first saw combat use around Christmas 1944 in the Ardennes. Priority for the M24 went to the cavalry reconnaissance squadrons, though the M24 was also issued to the armored divisions and separate tank battalions as they became available. This was arguably the best light tank of World War II, with the firepower of a medium tank.

E **DUEL IN COLOGNE, MARCH 6, 1945 (OVERLEAF)**
On March 6, the tanks of Task Force Doan, 3rd Armored Division entered Cologne. The Panther tank of Oberleutnant Wilhelm Bartelborth, the commander of 2.Zug, Pz.Abt.2106 of Panzerbrigade 106 "Feldherrnhalle" was lurking behind the city's famous cathedral. The Panther fired down Komödienstrasse, knocking out an advancing M4A3 tank. In the meantime, a T26E3 Pershing commanded by Sgt Robert Early of E/32nd Armored was moving down An den Dominikanern Strasse towards the cathedral. Bartelborth's Panther tank had advanced past the front of the cathedral to control the several streets leading into the plaza. The two tanks confronted each other at point blank range. Early's Pershing managed to fire three rounds before the Panther could respond, and the Panther erupted in flames from a catastrophic ammunition fire. Three crewmen escaped the burning Panther, though one died shortly after.

M24 light tank strength in ETO 1945					
	Jan	Feb	Mar	Apr	May
2nd AD			17	17	33
3rd AD			13	17	46
4th AD				17	24
5th AD			17	17	17
6th AD					20
7th AD			17	30	51
8th AD		82	82	79	82
9th AD				16	51
11th AD					18
13th AD					79
14th AD					5
16th AD				83	83
20th AD				83	83
Sub-total Armored Division		82	146	359	592
Tank battalions	20	34	67	71	97
Cavalry recon squadrons		12	150	302	455
Total	20	128	363	732	1,144

*Data from beginning of month

The M10 3in Gun Motor Carriage (GMC) formed the basis for self-propelled tank destroyer battalions through most of 1944. It was supplemented by the M18 76mm GMC from the summer of 1944. The main advantage of the M18 was its greater speed, a feature much prized by the misbegotten tank destroyer tactical doctrine of 1942–43. By 1943, this feature was recognized as being marginal at best to the tank destroyer mission. The most important feature was the ability to defeat German tanks, and neither the M10 nor M18 had adequate firepower against the frontal armor of the Panther or Tiger. The M36 90mm GMC finally began to appear in the ETO in October 1944, and it was the only US AFV with the ability to penetrate the heavier German tanks until the advent of the T26E3 heavy tank. Its performance became even better with the arrival of HVAP (high velocity armor piercing) ammunition in 1944. HVAP was available in limited quantities due to its dependence on a tungsten carbide core, as this alloy

1. T26E3 PERSHING, 18TH TANK BATTALION, 8TH ARMORED DIVISION, PLZEŇ, CZECHOSLOVAKIA, MAY 1945

During the short-lived occupation of the western Czech provinces in the late spring of 1945, the US Army V Corps conducted a number of parades in Czech towns. This T26E3 has been cleaned up and painted in colorful markings, including the vehicle name on the barrel "Bugs," the slogan "Alles Kaput" on the side stowage, and the unit's Black Panther insignia on the glacis plate and rear mud guard. The vehicle registration number is painted around the base of the turret, while the tactical unit insignia, 8^18^ B-9, is painted on the gun mantlet.

2. M24 LIGHT TANK, F TROOP, 2ND CAVALRY RECONNAISSANCE SQUADRON (MECHANIZED), BAVARIA, GERMANY, APRIL 1945

This tank is named after the famous movie star, Rita Hayworth, and is finished in the usual overall lusterless olive drab. This unit, which was attached to Patton's Third Army, painted the Third Army insignia on their turret during the final weeks of the war, a blue disc with red trim and a white letter A.

Two separate tank battalions were converted to special mine exploder battalions in late 1944. This is an M4A1 tank equipped with a T1E2 mine roller of the 739th Tank Battalion (SMX), attached to the Ninth US Army during the 1945 campaigns.

A Sherman IC 17pdr of the 8th Princess Louise (New Brunswick) Hussars, 5th Canadian Armoured Division, moving through Ijsselmeer on the Dutch coast on April 18, 1945 during the final campaign to liberate the Netherlands. As was common in 21st Army Group, the tank is covered in spare Churchill track links for protection against Panzerfaust. The 17pdr gun has a false muzzle break and white undershading to disguise its long gun barrel. (LAC PA-131043)

was in very short supply due to its widespread use in critical metal-working machine tools in the US. Usually, each M36 would receive a few rounds of HVAP. The HVAP ammunition also became available for the M10 and M18 in the late summer of 1944, and was used in the M4A1 and M4A3 tanks with the 76mm gun as well.

In the summer of 1944, self-propelled tank destroyer battalions were equipped with either the M10 or the M18; there were no mixed organizations. When the M36 became available in October 1944, it was generally issued to M10 battalions. Some battalions gradually converted entirely to the M36. The towed 3in tank destroyer battalions were generally reequipped with the M18 after the decision was made following the Ardennes campaign to abandon this flawed concept.

British/Canadian Armies

The remarkable feature of the tank inventory of the 21st Army Group was its sheer variety. This was in part due to the mixture of British-manufactured types combined with Lend–Lease American types. In addition, the British Army was very reluctant to retire older tank types. As mentioned in NVG 294 *Allied Tanks in Normandy 1944*, the 21st Army Group tended to maintain an unusually large number of tanks in reserve, sufficient to endure tank casualties of 25 percent per month.

The predominant tank in British/Canadian service in 1945 was the Sherman and in particular the Sherman V (M4A4). The vast majority of M4A4 production went to Britain, and it formed the basis for half of the six British/Canadian armoured

divisions in 1945 (Guards, 4th and 5th Canadian). The 7th Armoured Division was equipped primarily with the Cromwell, while the 11th Armoured Division was gradually reequipped with the new Comet by the end of the war. Even those armoured divisions not equipped primarily with the Sherman V tended to have some Sherman IC or VC 17pdr Fireflies. Overall, the Sherman represented about half the tank inventory of the 21st Army Group.

The best of the Shermans was arguably the Sherman IC and Sherman VC 17pdr Firefly, up-gunned with the 17pdr gun. This weapon was in high demand in 1944 due to the extensive tank fighting around Caen from June to August 1944. However, the level of tank-vs.-tank fighting by the 21st Army Group drastically declined after September, since its main opponent, Heeresgruppe H, had so few Panzers. The 17pdr, like the American 76mm gun, was optimized for antiarmor performance. Its high-explosive capability was mediocre. As a result, it was not as well suited to the engagement of non-armored targets, such as enemy troops and equipment that predominated in the 1945 fighting. This led to the retention of the 75mm Shermans, since they fired a heavier high-explosive round, better suited for dealing with non-armored targets.

A Sherman IIA of the 24 Pułk Ułanów, 1 Dywizja Pancerna (24th Lancer Regiment, 1st Polish Armoured Division) crosses a Bailey bridge during operations near the Küsten canal on April 19, 1945. The Polish division was the only element of 21st Army Group to use the M4A1 (76mm), and here it is seen fitted with spare tracks as applique armor to protect against Panzerfaust rockets.

An unusual equipment problem cropped up in September 1943 when the US halted manufacture of the M4A4 tank. Britain was obliged to accept some of the M4A1 (76mm), since the US Army had dibs on the M4A3 (76mm) as its preferred type. To avoid logistics issues in the 21st Army Group, only the Polish 1st Armoured Division was reequipped with this type.

British and Canadian forces faced the same problem as the US Army with regards to the proliferation of German antitank rocket launchers. However, the local solution was different. The 21st Army Group preferred to weld spare track links onto their tanks as applique armor.

Two British-manufactured tanks, the Churchill and Cromwell, made up about a third of the 21st Army Group's inventory. The Cromwell was the principal alternative to the Sherman for armoured divisions, equipping the 7th and 11th Armoured Divisions until the latter was re-equipped with the new Comet. Another major user of the Cromwell was the Czech Armoured Brigade. The new Comet tank was a further evolution of the Cromwell series, but armed with a 77mm gun. This weapon was derived from the 75mm gun, re-bored for a new type of ammunition that used the same projectile as the 17pdr, but with a smaller propellant case. The Comet was the best British tank of the war, but its use was largely confined to the 11th Armoured Division.

The Churchill infantry tank remained in service through to the end of the war, primarily in three armoured brigades (6th Guards, 31st and 34th). It was well suited to the type of infantry-support missions that predominated in the final months of the war. One of its most common variants was the Crocodile flamethrower tank, much prized to deal with German fortifications.

The British unit most closely associated with the Cromwell tank was the "Desert Rats," the 7th Armoured Division. This is a view of the 8th King's Royal Irish Hussars, the divisional armored reconnaissance regiment, in Brunen, Germany on March 27, 1945 following the Operation *Plunder* crossing of the Rhine. At least two Challenger 17pdr tanks and a few Shermans can be seen among the Cromwells.

Valentine infantry tanks, primarily the Valentine IX/X with the 6pdr and the XI with the 75mm gun, were used in small numbers as "chargers" by senior officers in the antitank regiments of the infantry divisions. These tanks shared the same chassis as the Valentine 17pdr tank destroyers used in these regiments.

The Stuart was the most common light tank in service, primarily the Stuart V (M3A3) and Stuart VI (M5A1). A small number of Chaffee entered service in the final weeks of the war with the 7th, Guards, and 4th Canadian Armoured Divisions.

By 1945, most M10 3in GMCs had been retired from the antitank regiments in favor of the M10 17pdr. This vehicle was the predominant type in the antitank regiments of the six armoured divisions of the 21st Army Group. The antitank regiments of the infantry divisions used the new Valentine 17pdr, better known after the war as the Archer.

Prior to the Rhine operations in March 1945, existing inventories of Valentine and Sherman DD (Duplex Drive) amphibious tanks were repaired and brought back into service. The Valentines were used primarily for training purposes, not tactical use.

G

1. SHERMAN V, 8TH PRINCESS LOUISE (NEW BRUNSWICK) HUSSARS, 5TH CANADIAN ARMOURED DIVISION, NETHERLANDS, APRIL 1945

Canadian Sherman tanks were finished in either the original US Army olive drab, or its British equivalent, SCC 15. Most of this tank's insignia has been obscured by the extensive array of Churchill track links welded to the tank as added anti-Panzerfaust protection. All that is evident is the white 52 on red square, indicating the second regiment in precedence within the brigade.

2. SHERMAN VC 17PDR, 24 PUŁK UŁANÓW, 1 DYWIZJA PANCERNA, GERMANY, APRIL 1945

Polish Fireflies were usually finished in overall British SCC 15 olive drab, since the tanks were often repainted from their original US olive drab after the conversion process. Most tactical markings are covered up by the addition of metal Sherman track or the ammunition boxes welded on to the bustle for added stowage. On the rear, two insignia are still evident, the national PL in a circle, and the division's winged hussar insignia.

1

2

21st Army Group tank/AFV status in 1945						
	27 Jan			**5 May**		
	Unit	Other	Sub-total	Unit	Other	Sub-total
Churchill III 6pdr	43	5	48	8	17	25
Churchill IV 6pdr	68	79	147	45	58	103
Churchill III 75mm	19	5	24	5	11	16
Churchill IV 75mm	104	39	143	57	35	92
Churchill VI 75mm	119	136	255	143	137	280
Churchill VII 75mm	34	131	165	75	143	218
Churchill Crocodile	86	41	127	154	35	189
Churchill V 95mm	62	38	100	59	18	77
Churchill VIII 95mm	0	0	0	1	7	8
Churchill AVRE	168	213	381	181	126	307
Churchill OP	22	1	23	16	0	16
Valentine IX/X	3	46	49	32	8	40
Valentine XI	0	61	61	53	22	75
Valentine DD	0	0	0	0	16	16
Valentine 17pdr	82	92	174	210	115	325
Sherman I	106	75	181	63	99	162
Sherman II	164	71	235	106	57	163
Sherman III	193	193	386	220	333	553
Sherman V	595	370	965	708	329	1037
Sherman IIA	135	51	186	142	149	291
Sherman IB	0	8	8	64	30	94
Sherman IC	408	357	765	485	295	780
Sherman VC	228	180	408	224	231	455
Sherman III DD	0	30	30	11	8	19
Sherman V DD	54	64	118	37	50	87
Sherman Crab	140	95	235	101	89	190
Sherman OP	107	76	183	222	60	282
M10	22	14	36	0	0	0
M10 17pdr	218	158	376	292	125	417
Cromwell IV/V	531	267	798	462	225	687
Cromwell VII	14	17	31	0	0	0
Cromwell VI	58	56	114	87	58	145
Cromwell OP	44	4	48	69	7	76
Challenger	22	29	51	30	63	93
Comet	102	2	104	237	226	463
Locust	0	0	0	9	88	97
Stuart III	38	64	102	38	17	55
Stuart V	13	106	119	122	59	181
Stuart VI	395	174	569	441	228	669
Chaffee	0	0	0	22	66	88
	4,397	**3,348**	**7,745**	**5,231**	**3,640**	**8,871**

BATTLE ANALYSIS

Allied tank casualties during the campaign in Germany differed markedly.
The British/Canadian 21st Army Group suffered nearly 3,000 tank and AFV
casualties in 1944, but only about half as many in 1945. This was in large

measure due to the intense tank-vs.-tank fighting endured by the British/Canadian tank units in Normandy around Caen in the summer of 1944 compared to the very limited tank-vs.-tank fighting in 1945.

British/Canadian 21st Army group tank losses			
	1944	**1945**	**total**
Stuart III/V	201	47	248
Stuart VI	80	105	185
Chafee	0	2	2
Sherman	1,855	857	2,712
Cromwell	464	145	609
Challenger	18	21	39
Comet	0	26	26
Churchill	365	291	656
Total	**2,983**	**1,494**	**4,477**

In contrast, US Army tank and AFV losses in 1944 and 1945 were roughly similar: 3,596 in 1944 and 3,623 in 1945. This was due to relatively modest losses in Normandy, the intensified tank combat in the Ardennes in late 1944 and early 1945, and the larger scale of US tank deployment in 1945.

BELOW LEFT
Due to the heavy casualties inflicted by Panzerfausts during the Operation *Nordwind* fighting in Alsace in January 1945, in February 1945, the Seventh US Army began a systematic program to retrofit their tanks with a standardized sand-bag applique contained in special metal frames welded to the tank. This M4 is a command tank of the 25th Tank Battalion, 14th Armored Division with a second radio mount, and was photographed in Huttendorf on February 11, 1945.

BELOW RIGHT
Patton was convinced by his ordnance officers that sand-bags were an inefficient means of protection. Instead, in February 1945, Third US Army stripped armor plate off derelict American and German tank wrecks in the Ardennes, and welded the plates to their tanks.

US Army tank and AFV losses in the ETO, 1945						
	Jan	Feb	Mar	Apr	May	total
Light tanks	208	93	136	190	112	739
M8 HMC	46	9	9	19	23	106
M4	585	320	463	554	207	2,129
M4 (105)	29	62	0	13	5	109
M18	27	16	21	55	21	140
M10	69	106	27	37	37	276
M36	26	18	21	34	25	124
Total	**990**	**624**	**677**	**902**	**430**	**3,623**

Compared to the campaigns in Normandy in 1944 or the Ardennes in 1944–45, the diminished strength of the Wehrmacht made Panzers a much less potent threat in 1945 than they had been previously. The proportion of Allied tank losses caused by German tanks and AFVs was not recorded in any detail, and other types of weapons were presumably responsible for a larger proportion of the casualties.

From the Allied perspective, towed and stationary German antitank guns posed a far greater threat than German tanks and AFVs. In February 1945, there were about 775 towed 7.5cm PaK 40 antitank guns and 130 towed 8.8cm PaK antitank guns assigned to German infantry divisions and supporting units of OB West. A total of 1,400 fixed 5cm, 7.5cm and 8.8cm antitank guns had been assigned to the West-Stellung defense lines along the Rhine, of which about 550 were emplaced by February 1945.[2] As a result, there were about 1,455 antitank guns along the Westfront in February 1945 compared to less than 900 operational German tanks and AFVs. While the number of towed and static antitank guns continued to increase in March and April 1945, there was a steady decline in operational tank and AFV strength.

German infantry antitank rocket weapons became a growing threat in 1945.[3] German infantry and Volksgrenadier regiments had a nominal allotment of 36 crew-served 8.8cm Panzerschreck launchers, compared to a dozen towed 7.5cm PaK 40 antitank guns. The smaller Panzerfaust rocket-propelled antitank grenade was far more numerous, with typically more than 500 issued to each regiment. By 1945, OB West's 56 infantry and Volksgrenadier divisions had only about a third of the authorized towed 7.5cm PaK 40 antitank guns, and antitank rocket launchers often served as a substitute.

Allied accounts do not distinguish between Panzerschreck and Panzerfaust encounters. But it is evident from operational research conducted at the time that these rocket antitank weapons became an increasing threat in the later months of the 1945 campaign.

A Panther Ausf. G, possibly from 9.Panzer Division, overrun by CCB, 11th Armored Division in the village of Kelberg during the Third US Army's Rhineland offensive, March 7, 1945. From the towing bars in front of the tank, it was probably broken down and awaiting recovery. Records of 53.Korps suggest that the few tanks in the area were out of fuel and ammunition at the time.

2   Steven Zaloga, *Defense of the Rhine 1944–45*, Osprey Fortress 102, (2011)
3   Steven Zaloga, *Panzerfaust vs. Sherman: European Theater 1944–45*, Osprey Duel 99, (2019)

Allied tank casualties in ETO by Panzerfaust/Panzerschreck 1944–45				
(percentage of total tank casualties)				
Jan 45	Feb	Mar	Apr	May
6	4	15	24	41

The growing percentage of tank losses to antitank rockets was due to several factors. Panzerfaust production increased six-fold from August 1944 to February 1945, rising from 250,000 monthly to 1.5 million. The Panzerfaust proved especially troublesome to Allied tanks during the urban fighting in German towns and cities, as well as in close terrain such as forest. The growing importance of the Panzerfaust was also due to the sharp decline in the number of German tanks and conventional antitank guns in the final two months of the war.

Percentage of British tanks lost to Panzerfaust/Panzerschreck			
Campaign	Tanks KO'd (Knocked Out)	KO'd by shaped charge	Percentage of losses
Normandy (Jun–Sep 44)	83	5	6%
Belgium and Holland (Sep 44 – 8 Feb 45)	76	7	9%
Germany, west of Rhine (8 Feb – 24 Mar 45)	30	2	7%
Germany, east of Rhine (24 Mar – 3 May 45)	274	94	34%

FURTHER READING

There are no survey histories of tank combat in the West in 1945. There are numerous specialized studies of the various types of tanks and AFVs involved in these campaigns, but the focus tends to be on their technical aspects and not their tactical employment. Campaign and unit histories deal with the operational aspects of tank employment, but usually at a very general level. Many of these books were consulted for this work, but they are too numerous to list here. This book also was prepared using archival resources, especially for the statistical data presented here. The data came primarily from the US National Archives and Records Administration (NARA II) in College Park, MD, particularly RG 407 for US Army records and RG 242 for German records. British statistics came from both NARA II and The National Archives in Kew.

The soggy ground conditions in the Roer area were a major tactical hazard during Operation *Grenade* in late February 1945. This M36 90mm GMC of the 703rd Tank Destroyer Battalion, 3rd Armored Division is completely bogged down in muddy fields near Buir, Germany on February 26, 1945 while the crew waits for a recovery vehicle to help extricate it. The vehicle's .50 cal machine gun has been moved to a more useful position in the front of the turret instead of the factory location on the bustle.

INDEX

Figures in **bold** refer to illustrations.

AFV (Armored Fighting Vehicle) 4, 7, 12, 15, **A16**, 26, 28, 29, 38, 44–7
Allied Forces 4–7, 9, 12, 14, **C24**, 28–30, 44, 46–7
Alsace, 5–7, **8**, **10**, **14**, **18**, 19, **B20**, 23, **29**, 45
Ardennes attack/offensive 5–7, 13, 15–16, 20, 22–3, 26–8, 32–5, 40, **45**, 46
armored cars/vehicles 4, 12, 23, 29
artillery **10**, 33–4
  field 4, 19–20, 24
assault gun (*Sturmgeschütz*) 4, 18, 28

Bastogne 6, 20
Belgium 7, 22, 47
Berlin 6–8, 12
Blitzkrieg 20, 23
Bradley, Gen. Omar 5–6, 9, 11–12, 20
Britain 19, 40–1
British Army 5, **C24**, 30, 40
  British Second Army 11, 13, 24
  12th Army Group 16
  21st Army Group 5, 8–10, 13, 16, 23, 24, 26, 40, 41, 42, 44–5
  armoured brigades
    29th **C24**; 31st 26, 41; 34th 26, 41
  armoured divisions
    7th 23, 41–2; 11th 23, **C24**, 41; 79th 10, 22, 24
  Governor General's Foot Guards 23, 41–2

Caen 41, 45
camouflage **A16**, **C24**, **D30**
Canadian Army: First Canadian Army 13, 24; armoured divisions: 4th **23**, 41–2; 5th 23, 41
casemate 27
  fixed 27, 30
Cologne 4, 8, **14**, 15, **30**, **34**, **E35**
Czechoslovakia 13, **F38**
  Czech Armoured Brigade 26, 41

Devers, Lt Gen. Jacob 5–6, 13, 19

Eisenhower, Gen. Dwight 4, 8, 10, 12–13
ETO (European Theater of Operations) 19, 22–3, 32–3, 35, 38, 46–7

French Army 23
  1re Armée Française (First French Army) 6, 23; 2e Division Blindée 8, **B20**, 23

German Army: Korpsgruppe Bayerlein 5, 15
  5. Panzer-Armee 15, 20
  6.SS-Panzer-Armee 7, 13
  Panzer-Brigade.106 (Pz.Bde.106) 9, 15
  Panzer-Brigade Westfalen 16, 18, 28
  Panzer-Division: 2.Panzer-Division (2.Pz. Div.) 9, 13
  9.Panzer-Division (9.Pz.Div.) 9, 13, **15**, **27**
  11.Panzer-Division (11.Pz.Div.) 4, 9, 13, 15, **A16**
  21.Panzer-Division (21.Pz.Div.) 14
  116.Panzer-Division (116.Pz.Div.) 8–10, 13
  Panzer-Flamm-Kompanie.352 19, **29**
  Panzergrenadier-Bataillon (*gepanzerte*) 15
  Panzergrenadier-Division:
    3.Panzergrenadier-Division (3.Pz.Gren.Div.) 9, 13
    15.Panzergrenadier-Division (15.Pz.Gren. Div.) 9–10, 13
    17.SS-Panzergrenadier-Division (17.SS-Pz. Gren.Div.) 9, 13
    25.Panzergrenadier-Division **29**
  Panzerjäger-Abteilungen (tank destroyer battalions) **10**, **12**, **15**, **18**, 19, 22, **23**, 38, 40, **47**
  s.Pz.Abt.(FKL).301 9, 15–16, 28, **45**
  schwere Panzerjäger Abteilung (heavy tank destroyer battalion) (s.Pz.Jg.Abt.): 506 9, 15–16, 28; 653 **8**, **12**, 18; 654 **8**, **12**,

18, **D30**
Panzer-Lehr Division (Pz.Lehr.Div.) 5, 13, 15, 9, **A16**
  I./Pz.Lehr-Rgt.130 12
  Waffen-SS 13, 16
  Wehrmacht 4–7, 9, 12–13, **A16**, 26–8, 46
  Volksgrenadier 14, 18, 29, 46
Germany 4–5, 6, 7, 13, **A16**, **B20**, **C24**, 26, 27, 28–9, **D30**, **F38**, **G42**, 44, 47
Gun Motor Carriage (GMC) **8**, **12**, **15**, **23**, 38, 42, 47

half-tracks 4, 15, 23, 29
Heeresgruppe:
  B 5, 9, 11–12, 15
  G 5–6, 9, 13
  H 5, 41
Hitler, Adolf 6, 9, 12, **29**
HVAP (high velocity armor piercing) 38, 40
HVSS (horizontal volute spring suspension) 33, **34**, 35

Korpsgruppe Bayerlein 5, 15
Kriegsstärkenachweisungen: (war-establishment strength) (KStN) 13–15

Model, Generalfeldmarschall Walter 5, 12
Montgomery, Field Marshal Bernard 5, 8–10, 12, **13**, **23**, 24

Netherlands (Holland) 5, 13, **16**, 40, **G42**, 47
Normandy 4, 45–7
Norway 6, 11, **28**

OB West (*Oberbefehlshaber West* (High Command West)) 5, 8–9, 12–15, 18–19, 26, 28–30, 46
operations:
  Blockbuster 8, **23**
  Enterprise 13
  Flashpoint 10
  Grenade 34
  Lumberjack 8, 10, **12**, 16
  Nordwind 6, 19, **29**, 45
  Overlord 4
  Plunder 42
  Queen 5
  Undertone 8, 10
  Varsity-Plunder 8–10
  Veritable 6, 8
  Voyage 11
Ostfront (Russian Front) 4, 7, 13, 18, 29

Paderborn 11, 16, 18
Panzerfaust rocket-propelled antitank grenade 34, 46–7
Panzerschreck rocket launchers 18, 34, 46–7
Panzerwaffe 26, 28
Patton, General George S. 10–11, 13, 15, **19**, 34, **35**, **F38**, **45**

Red Army, the 6–7, 13
Remagen bridgehead 4, 5, 10–11, **D30**
rivers:
  Elbe 11, 13, 16
  Rhine 5, 6, 8–10, **19**, **23**, **24**, **26**, 34, **42**, 46, 47
  Roer 5, 8, 9, 15–16, **47**
  rocket launchers 18, **33**, 34, 41, 46
  Ruhr 11–12, 20, 28

Saar 5–7, 9–10, 13, 33

tanks: 7.5cm Sfl 8, 19
  BergePz. 11
  Beute Pz. 11
  Chaffee 26, 35, 42, 44
  Churchill 10, 12, 24, **26**, 40, 41, **G42**, 44–5
  Comet **C24**, 41, 44–5
  Crab flail 24
  Cromwell **24**, 26, 30, 32, 41, **42**, 44–5

Duplex Drive (DD):
  M4A1 **4**, **19**, 33–4, 40, **41**
  M4A2 **B20**, 33–4
  M4A3 **B20**, 33, 34, **E35**, 40–1
  M4A3E2 **9**, **B20**, 35
  M4A3E8 **33**, **34**
  M4A4 33–4, 40–1
  M5A1 **20**, **22**, 23, 33, 35, 42
  Fireflies 41, **G42**
  Flak Pz. 9, 11
  Kingtiger 32
  Locust 10, 26
  M24 Chaffee **22**, 33, 35, **F38**; M8 23, **33**, 46
  mine-clearing 24
Panther 6–9, **11**, 13, **15**, **A16**, 19, 27–9, **E35**, 38
  Ausf. D 16
  Ausf. G 5, **12**, **15**, **A16**, 32, **46**
Panzer 5–11, 13–16, 19–20, 23, 26, 28
  Pz.II 6
  Pz.III 6, 8, 11, 19
  Pz.IV 8, 11, 19
  Pz.IV Lg (A) 7
  Pz.IV Lg (V) 7
  Pz.IV/70 9, 11, 15, 18, **27**, 28–9
  Pz.IV/70 (A) 27
  Pz.IV/70 (V) **14**, 27
  PzKpfw IV Ausf. G 4
  PzKpfw IV Ausf. H 27, 30, 32
  PzKpfw IV Ausf. J **14**, 27
  PzKpfw III Ausf. N **16**, 28
  PzKpfw 38 (t) 28
  Pershing T26E3 **12**, **27**, 33, **E35**, **E38**, 45
  Sherman **11**, **23**, 24, 26, 30, 32, 34, 40, 41, **G42**, 44–5; M4 **13**, 32–4, 45, 46
  Stuart 26, 42, 44–5
  StuG 6–9, 11, **15**, **16**, 18–19, **27**, 28–9
  StuH 11
  Sturmpanzer 7–8, 18–19
  Tiger 6–9, 11, 15–16, 18–19, 28–9, **D30**, 32, 35, 38, **45**
  Valentine 6, **C24**, 26, 42, 44
tank destroyers (*Panzerjäger*) 4, 6, 8, **12**, 15, 18, 20, 22, **23**, 27, 29, 33, 38, 42
  Jagdpanther 7–8, 11, **12**, 18–19, 29, **D30**
  Jagdpanzer 38 (Jagd.Pz.38) 7, 11, **18**, 19, 28, **29**
  Jagdtiger 7–8, 10, 11, 18–19, 29
  M10 **6**, **8**, **15**, 26, 40, 42, 44
  M18 33, 38, 40, 46
  M36 **12**, 33, 38, 40, 46, 47
Nashorn 8, 11, 18–19, 29
TO&E (table of organization and equipment) 19, 22–3

US Army 6, 8, 11, 18–20, 22–3, 32–5, **F38**, 41, **G42**, 45–7
  Army Ground Forces 19, 22, 33
  6th Army Group 5–6, 8–9, 13
  12th Army Group 5–6, 9, 11, 16, **20**, 32–3
  First US Army 8, 10–11, 20, 22
  Ninth US Army 8, 10–11, 20, 22, 34, 40
  Seventh US Army 6, 33–4, 45
  Third US Army 10–11, 13, 15, **19**, 34, **35**, **45**, 46
  armored divisions:
    1st 19; 2nd 11, 12, 19–20, 32, 34; 3rd 4, 11, 14, 18–20, 27, 32, 34, **E35**, 45, 47; 4th 32, 34; 5th 32; 6th **B20**, 32, 34; 7th 13, 32, 41; 8th 32, **F38**; 9th 10, 12, 32; 10th 32; 11th 32, 41, 46; 12th 32–4; 13th 32; 14th 32, 34, 45; 16th 32; 20th 32
33rd Armored Regiment 4, 27, 45
  tank battalions:
    25th **45**; 712th 34; 736th 22, 34; 738th 22; 739th 22, **40**; 740th 22; 743rd 33; 746th 9; 748th **19**, 34; 753rd 34; 761st 20; 781st 34

Westfront (Western Front) 4, 6, 45–6